SUCCESSFUL JUMPING

Training Your Horse with Gridwork

Successful Jumping

TRAINING YOUR HORSE WITH GRIDWORK

Karen Bush and Ross Irving

The Crowood Press

First published in 1993 by
The Crowood Press Ltd
Ramsbury, Marlborough
Wiltshire SN8 2HR

British Library Cataloguing-in-Publication Data

A catalogue record for this book is available from the British Library.

ISBN   1 85223 763 5

Acknowledgements
The authors would like to thank Bob and Kay De Luca for the use of their
facilities for the photograph sessions, plus all those who kindly agreed to be
the models! Also thanks to Country Jumpkins for permission to use the
photograph on page 87 and to MVR Photographic for the photographs on
pages 15, 131 and 148 (top).
Artworks by Hazel Morgan.

Author's Note
Readers may notice that in some of the photographs the riders are not always
wearing fitted chinstraps on their hard hats; although this is a matter of
personal preference when working at home, we would like to stress that riding,
and especially jumping, is a high-risk activity, and we would strongly
recommend that headgear meeting current BS specifications is always worn; at
shows nowadays it is indeed compulsory to do so anyway.

Throughout this book, 'he', 'him' and 'his' have been used as neutral pronouns
and as such refer to both males and females.

Typeset by Chippendale Type Ltd, Otley, West Yorkshire.
Printed and bound in Great Britain by Redwood Books, Trowbridge.

Contents

Introduction

Every horse has a certain amount of aptitude for jumping – some more than others – but it is up to you as the rider to produce and train it to its full potential. A common misconception is that schooling over fences can increase the horse's inherent ability (it won't), but sensible and correctly managed training will at least enable the horse to realize fully what talent it has.

One of the best ways of achieving this, whether teaching a younger horse to jump or trying to improve the technique and attitude of a more mature animal, is through the use of poles on the ground and grids of fences. Unfortunately, for many people, the subject of 'gridwork', 'athletic' or 'gymnastic' jumping (all terms used to describe basically the same sort of work) is often baffling and shrouded in mystery. There is in fact nothing mysterious about it at all; it is simply a logical system of training, which, provided you have a good measure of common sense and some empathy or 'feel' for the way the horse is going, can offer a number of benefits:

• It helps to muscle up the horse without the necessity of pushing it over huge fences and risking overfacing it too early in its career.
• It builds up confidence in both horse and rider.
• It teaches the horse to think for itself and allows it to learn from making its own mistakes.
• It speeds up the rider's reflexes and helps him to develop an eye for a stride.
• It can improve the horse's technique so that it jumps more cleanly, accurately and economically.
• It teaches the horse to deal with combinations of fences, which it will have to do in competition.
• It encourages a more positive attitude in horse and rider.
• It helps to avoid boredom and discourages bad habits which might arise from jumping only single fences.
• To a certain extent, it can be used to correct bad habits.

All the exercises in this book progress in a logical sequence; if your horse is a youngster, has acquired bad habits, or has never done gridwork before (and never assume that it has) it would obviously be sensible to follow them through in this order. Never be afraid to go back a stage or two if the horse has been laid off or develops a problem, and do not underestimate the value of using simpler grids as a warm-up for a more experienced horse or as a preparation for introducing a new exercise. Never begin a lesson with anything new, but establish confidence first with the familiar, reminding your horse of what it learnt the last time. Do not feel that you have to introduce a new exercise every work session either, but take time to consolidate each stage before moving on to the next, rather than risk losing what you have achieved. With a talented horse, it can frequently be tempting to try to push on more quickly, and this is all too often when problems occur.

Gridwork should be used to serve a purpose, so to some extent it does need to be tailored to suit each individual horse. It is therefore somewhat impractical simply to lay out a rigid format of exercises which may not be entirely suitable for or relevant to some horses. This book does provide some examples of grids, but the idea behind it is primarily to explain the basic principles and logical progression involved in such gymnastic work. You will then be able to apply that knowledge to building grids that will be of most benefit to your own horse, rather than just using generalized exercises to less effect.

Of course, despite all your best efforts and intentions, problems can crop up for one reason or another, so a 'troubleshooting' chapter has also been included at the end of the book (*see* page 125). This will help you to identify the most likely causes of difficulty and determine a remedy.

1 Using Gridwork

AIMS

The aim of 'gymnastic' or 'athletic' jumping work using grids of fences is fairly straightforward: it is to encourage the horse to use itself in a more athletic way so that it can realize its full potential. If, for example, the horse is very stiff and hollow over fences, it is unlikely that it will be able to lift and tuck up its feet correctly; thus it will need to make a bigger effort and jump higher than is really necessary. Although a fence may be only 90cm (3ft) in height, the horse's style of jumping may mean that it is actually having to jump 1.4m (4ft 6in) in height in order to clear it. By teaching it to develop a more athletic style, the horse can be a little more economical with its energy and may be able to tackle larger fences more successfully. It will also be less likely to roll poles off than if its legs are dangling beneath it.

In addition to developing a better style or technique in the air, there are other benefits to be gained from gymnastic jumping work: it will teach the horse to co-ordinate itself between fences and to tackle combinations with confidence, and both horse and rider will learn how to judge stride and distances to fences more accurately. The approach to a show jump is of the utmost importance, and one of the big advantages of gymnastic jumping using grids is that it helps you to bring your horse into each fence so that it meets it every time at the ideal take-off point. This puts the horse in a position where it has to use itself more correctly, thus increasing its chances of clearing it. Distances can be adjusted so that the individual horse can build up its confidence and experience. The fences themselves can be whatever size you wish; they do not have to be big in order to produce improvement. In fact, smaller fences correctly used can teach just as much while allowing you to smooth out any little problems or doubts without the danger of overfacing your horse. With a confident horse, introducing an occasional bigger fence will help to prevent complacency from setting in, but never feel that you have to keep building bigger and bigger obstacles.

When talking of gymnastic jumping, most people immediately think of gridwork, that is a line of fences set at related distances to each other, but the term does also cover single fences used in combination with trotting, canter, placing and landing poles. All horses are different, so one of the golden rules to remember when tackling gymnastic work is that it should be tailored specifically to each individual: an exercise or distance that is beneficial for one horse may not prove to be as successful or effective with another. Age, attitude, length of stride, experience, and any problems the horse has, must all be taken into account and must influence the types of fence you build, the distances between them, the placing of ground poles, and indeed the number of fences you include when building a grid (if, of course, a grid is appropriate).

Gridwork exercises are not ideal for all horses. The type likely to gain the most benefit is the young horse still learning its job. However, it can still be extremely useful with older horses, teaching those with a longer stride to shorten, and getting stuffier types to be quicker thinking and more agile (as well as all the other benefits already discussed). However, it is important to appreciate that gridwork will *not* work miracles and that it is better suited to some horses than others. With those whose temperaments incline them towards being very quick and sharp, a line of fences can actually speed them up even more and make them quicker and sharper, which is not really desirable. With this type of horse, it is probably best to use placing poles in front of fences, rather than a whole line of obstacles, to encourage a better approach and effort. It should also be said that you should not expect gymnastic work to make your horse more careful – either it is already or it never will be. However, by encouraging a better technique and approach, you will encourage the horse to jump more cleanly.

Finally, when assessing your goals, it is important to remember that an improvement in performance will only come over a period of time and with progressive training, not overnight, so be patient and do not imagine that gymnastic jumping is a short cut to achieving results.

TECHNIQUE

If a horse has reasonably good conformation it should have at least a certain amount of jumping ability. However, the style or technique with which a horse will tackle a fence can vary tremendously from one individual to another. If you look at a variety of top showjumpers, you will see the differences: some have a very classical style; others do not possess such good style, but because they are brave, careful and scopey, they are able to overcome their shortcomings in this respect, and do exceptionally well, winning a lot of classes.

The term 'technique' is basically another name for shape. The ideal shape that the horse should make over a fence is a perfect 'bascule' – that is, the appearance of a rounded (convex) curve from poll to tail with the point of shoulder swinging forward and upwards and the head lowered. This allows the forelegs to be tightly tucked up well out of the way so they clear the jump; it also allows the back end to follow through and be lifted above the poles. The impression of the horse 'rounding its back' is to a large extent an illusion: it is not actually possible for it physically to 'bend' its back along the saddle line because this area is of necessity fairly rigid. It has had to evolve in this way in order to cope with its lifestyle over thousands of years, and it is in fact this very rigidity which makes it possible for the horse to support the weight of a rider. As a herbivore, the horse has a capacious digestive tract which can deal with a large quantity of fibrous material in a more or less continuous state of digestion. This burdens the horse with a considerable weight to carry around. The spine has evolved to carry this weight, which at all times is pulling down on the vertebrae in the saddle area. So, when the horse is said to be 'rounding his back' over a fence, most of the flexion is really occurring at just two sites: the first joint of the thoracic

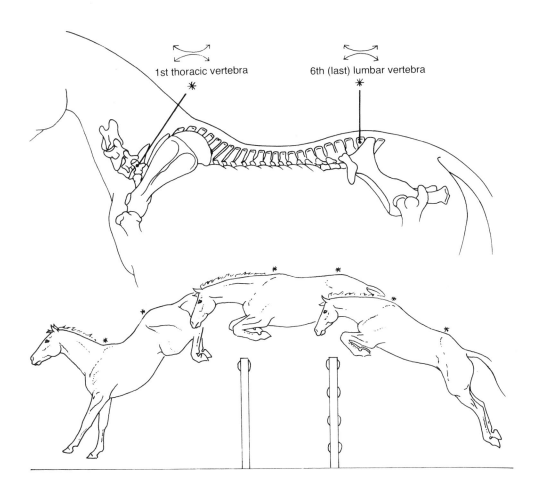

1st thoracic vertebra   6th (last) lumbar vertebra

The main points of flexion in the spine when jumping.

vertebrae (under the withers) and to a much greater extent at the joint between the last lumbar and the first of the sacral vertebrae (adjacent to the pelvis). The lowering of the head and neck enhances and contributes considerably to the appearance of a curved outline.

A horse that jumps in this rounded style will be a careful and fluent jumper as well as one that can afford to be economical in the height by which it clears a fence. The whole impression should be of its curling itself over a fence in the same way that a human high-jumper does.

Another reason why a good technique is such a desirable quality to cultivate is that jumping higher than necessary to clear a fence (overjumping) can easily frighten the horse – especially if it is a youngster – and can result in excessive jarring to the front legs on landing, as

The phases of the jump can be broken down into five stages.

Approach

Take-off

1 – APPROACH   The horse should arrive at the jump in a good balance and with a regular rhythm. The hocks should be well engaged beneath the body, providing impulsion. As the horse gets closer the head is lowered, gauging the height of the fence from the ground upwards. Just before the take-off, it is then raised again in order to help lift the forehand.

2 – TAKE-OFF   The horse sits back on to its hocks, away from the fence, to produce upwards and forwards propulsion. As the front feet are lifted from the ground the neck is shortened. The shoulders begin to swing forwards and the forearms are raised, knees bent and cannons tucked tightly back.

3 – FLIGHT   In profile, the horse should give an appearance of 'roundness' – the head and neck lowered and extended forwards to continue the arc shape of the topline. This lowering of the head and neck helps to draw the back end upwards and forwards over the fence; the back legs should be flexed slightly.

4 – LANDING   The horse lands with all its weight supported on one front leg, placing a considerable strain on it that increases with height and speed. As the horse lands, the head and neck are raised again to re-establish balance; by doing this, weight is transferred backwards and the forehand is able to remain as light and mobile as possible. The hindquarters are lowered, the back supple, so that the hind legs can come beneath the body.

5 – GETAWAY   Balance, impulsion and rhythm are re-established as quickly as possible, the hind legs engaged actively and pushing the horse forward for the next stride(s), or in preparation for the next fence. Even if a fence has been approached from trot, the horse should be encouraged to move away from it in canter.

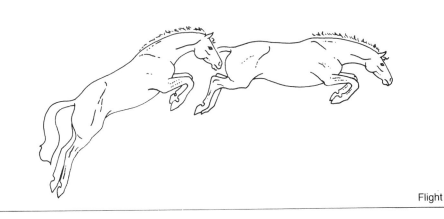

Flight

Landing

Getaway

well as being unpredictable and unseating for the rider.

How far you should go in attempting to alter radically your horse's style of jumping by using athletic exercises depends to a large extent on the material you are working with. A youngster is a clean slate and it is to be hoped that it will learn the correct way of working from the start, provided its education is properly managed along the right lines – nothing beats good foundations. A ten-year-old, on the other hand, can pose more of a problem. While a horse of this age is not too old to improve – and if taken back to scratch it is possible to iron out a lot of bad habits – this may take a lot of time and effort to achieve. Such a horse is also likely to be rather set in its ways, so if it is jumping double clear rounds in classes, going in a reasonable if not classical manner, and staying careful, it may ultimately be a wiser policy to leave well alone. Trying to change its technique completely – as opposed to tidying it up – can have an adverse effect in that it may become very confused and actually end up jumping less well than before. In such instances there may be more of a case for the rider changing his style to accommodate the horse rather than vice versa. Sometimes the rider can considerably influence for better or worse the way in which a horse jumps (*see* Chapter 7 p.101); for example, the horse may jump hollow because the rider repeatedly sits back and restricts with the reins, so it can often help to have an experienced person watch occasionally to help decide whether a less than desirable technique is more the rider's problem than the horse's.

It can be argued that it is not important what the horse looks like as long as it is clearing its fences. Nevertheless, it is advisable to try to get as near perfect a technique as possible if you do have a youngster (or younger horse), so as to make your work with it in the future easier. Again, this is often helped by having an experienced person to watch you. Alternatively, ask a friend to photograph or video you, as sometimes your horse may feel very good, but in reality may not be going as well as you thought. If you do encounter a problem, videos can in fact be a very useful way of analysing just what is going wrong: the same moment can be replayed endlessly, slowed down or even frozen until you have succeeded in pinpointing the source of the trouble.

Having said that, do be careful not to become too obsessed by what you see, as it can result in making you try too hard the next time, which can create more difficulties.

GUIDELINES

When tackling gymnastic work for the first time with your horse – whether it is a grid of fences or just a placing pole used to help it find the right take-off point – do not take it for granted that the horse has done such work before. Start off slowly; confronting the horse immediately with a complex problem to deal with will frighten it and be counter-productive.

● Always begin each session by spending some time loosening your horse up; no athlete would train without warming his muscles up first, and neither should your horse.
● If you suspect that your horse is

These two pictures show very well the sort of technique you do and don't want to encourage in the front end. Above, the horse is using itself extremely well, with its knees well up and the cannons tucked tightly back. Below, the shoulder has not swung up and forward, and nor has the forearm.
(Photos: courtesy of MVR Photographic.)

Do aim to keep your horse happy in its work. Be sensible in your aims and ambitions and you will find yourself having a lot more fun, too.

uncomfortable or struggling with an exercise, do not persist with it, but check your distances and if necessary go back a stage to confirm what the horse has already learned and boost its confidence.

• Horses learn by repetition and gain confidence from repeating lessons they know they can do well. So if your horse has a problem of some kind, backtrack to simpler, familiar exercises before progressing any further. If it has been off work or missed a few sessions, it is a good idea to start off with a little 'revision' anyway.

• Always establish and consolidate one exercise before going on to the next one,

but do not repeat it to the point of boring the horse or making it careless through complacency.

• Never spoil a lesson by overdoing things. If your horse has gone well and you have achieved your aims for that session after just ten minutes, do not feel you have to continue but leave it at that. End on a good note with a pat and a few words of praise. If the horse needs more work than you have given it, take it out for a hack instead.

• Try to avoid introducing too many new things in one lesson.

• Change the rein regularly so that neither of you becomes one-sided.

• Any exercise which is not achieving the result you want should be altered to be more constructive.

• It is best to set your distances so as to encourage your horse to get close to the fences as this will get it to sit back on its hocks and power itself upwards.

• Aim to educate, not to exhaust; gymnastic work can be very strenuous.

When using grids, the horse should be allowed to find its own way through them; just as children have to learn from experience and by making their own mistakes, so do horses. Grids allow them to do this without height, so that if they do make a mistake it need not be disastrous or frightening. Once you have jumped the first fence, allow your horse to keep going with the minimum of adjustment so that it learns to sort itself out. Up to three or four fences is probably the ideal number to include in a grid, and these should be placed in a straight line. Asking a horse to jump through a curved line requires the rider to interfere in order to bring the horse to the centre of each fence, and it would take fairly exceptional riding to be able to do this without increasing the pace.

True parallels are one of the most useful schooling fences as they encourage the horse to really use itself fully. In this picture, taken at a competition, the horse shows a very good technique, dropping its head nicely and ready to follow through with its back end.

The last thing you want to do in a grid is to touch the horse's mouth; rather, you should be aiming to lighten the contact and sit still, giving the horse the chance to think for itself.

For good technique in the air, you need to be able to ride to fences consistently at a steady pace, and with rhythm and impulsion as opposed to speed: the faster the pace, the less time the horse will have to look at and evaluate the obstacle, the flatter the jump will be and the less control or balance there will be on landing. If the horse has been used for cross-country work or hunting, it may well be inclined to jump from speed and will need to be slowed down in order to improve its technique. If the horse has become strong, too, it may resent this initially, and will need to do some basic flatwork and polework to re-educate it into thinking and working more steadily before tackling gymnastic jumping. With this sort of horse (or one that is inclined to speed up between fences and needs to be checked to prevent it from running away with you), it is usually a good idea to include fewer fences in a line rather than more, and to start off by approaching the first one from trot rather than canter; provided the horse has its hocks engaged beneath it, you will often be surprised by how big a fence it can jump from this pace.

One of the main causes of horses rushing their fences is the rider's nerves; not just when under pressure in a competition, but also if anticipating a problem when faced with a more difficult fence at home, or even when jumping a number of obstacles, as in a grid. It is all too easy for the rider to pick up the pace in his anxiety to get it over with as quickly as possible. As has been mentioned already, horses learn by repetition, and if they are constantly asked to jump too fast, they soon learn to flatten, and it eventually becomes a habit. It is always easier to speed up a horse than to teach it to slow down, so especially when training a youngster all its early work should be slow and steady, and great care should be taken not to over-ride him.

On the other side of the coin, horses that are not going forward properly should not be asked to jump complicated grids, and some time spent on improving its response to the leg on the flat would be sensible (*see* Chapter 4). When starting this type of horse off on simpler exercises – such as placing a pole in front of a fence – emphasis should still be placed on this aspect; if you find the horse is not making ground and going forward properly, give him a sharp smack with a stick just behind the girth as he is going over the pole. Continue to do this until the horse does achieve better forward motion, but do be careful nevertheless to take progress very steadily with a horse that is as laid back as this, because those which tend to spook and back off their fences before they get to them (as opposed to being downright lazy) are often the ones that turn out to be the good jumpers in the long run. There is no reason why you should not also click your tongue or even hiss at your horse to give him a bit more encouragement if necessary. The late and great Caroline Bradley was also a great believer in hissing at horses to get them to make more ground through combinations.

Do resist the temptation to ask more from the horse than it can give; if it makes a mistake and knocks a pole down, don't punish it. If the horse jumps it again afterwards (even unsuccessfully) but really tries hard and makes a good effort, then do praise it, because this is all you can reasonably ask for or expect – the best effort each horse can make. They may not progress further than Intermediate classes at unaffiliated shows, or they may turn out to be real stars, but either way they all need to be treated carefully. Overstretching or frightening the horse is very easily done, so, as the rider, you need to take note constantly of how he is coping and reacting in order to guide you as to how much to demand. If it feels as though the horse is jumping in two halves, freezing in the air, becoming very tight behind the saddle, or indeed, stopping, it is usually because the horse is trying to tell you something.

HOW OFTEN?

How often you jump and how much you ask depends entirely on the individual horse, on how it went previously, its experience, and on the weather. One of the biggest problems – unless you are lucky enough to have an all-weather surface – is posed by the ground: greasy going can cause the horse to slip about and lose confidence (although studs will help to a degree), while hard ground can jar the legs badly and cause soreness and loss of fluency, so you will need to be flexible in your training programme and choose days to jump when the going is suitable rather than make rigid plans to jump on specific days of the week. If the weather is appalling, do not feel that you have to be a martyr to the cause, either; after all, though you may have to cope with inclement weather conditions at shows, the idea of schooling over fences

Do not underestimate the value of allowing your horse to have a little time to itself to relax and unwind out in the field. If you are worried about the possibility of injuries then turn the horse out with a quiet companion and with protective boots on.

is to improve confidence and technique, and you are not going to achieve this with any great degree of success if your horse is not concentrating because of driving rain.

Gymnastic jumping is very demanding of both muscular effort and concentration, so only ask of your horse as much as he is mentally and physically capable of giving. Although it is a mistake to wait until a horse is fully mature to teach it everything (when it may have become too strong to deal with), do take care not to stretch youngsters too much. Remember that at four years they are not fully mature, and even at five they may still be growing. A small, compact horse will tend to mature more quickly than a big gangly one, which needs more time to grow into its larger frame; at five years old, it may be doing the same work as the smaller four-year-old. German horses also tend to mature more quickly than English or Irish breeds, so size and type may well have a bearing on how much to do.

It is often worth checking the time of year at which a youngster was born too; if it was a late foal, it could mean that it is actually six months younger than you thought, and although it may technically be a four-year-old, in real age it is only three-and-a-half. This sort of situation can often explain apparent immaturity and backwardness and will certainly influence the type and quantity of work you do.

Older horses can have problems, too, and may suffer from stiffness and arthritis with increasing years, so you will also need to consider their well-being. Obviously, correct work will help to loosen off any stiffness, but you may need to allow a longer warming-up period (particularly when the weather is cold). If the horse is unaccustomed to working athletically on the flat and over fences, you must be prepared to build it up gradually, not cripple the horse at the outset through your enthusiasm to improve him. Whether young or old, never work your horse to the point of tiredness, as this is when both physical and mental damage can be done.

You do not need to jump every day; variety is important and you should try to keep the work interesting by including other activities such as hacking and

Keep your work varied and include activities such as hacking to help keep your horse sweet in its outlook on life. However, it is well worth protecting your investment by putting knee-caps on your horse if you are planning to do any road work.

lungeing as well as flatwork and jumping. Some horses do need more jumping work than others, so to a large extent you must be guided by your instinct and knowledge of the individual horse, but the golden rule to remember is that everything should be done in moderation. Keep giving your horse that little bit more to do in its work each time, but ensure that it can always do what is asked of it comfortably, and allow it to enjoy its life and work.

2 Make and Shape

There is no such thing as a 'typical' showjumper. Scope and ability can come in any shape or form. One of the most fascinating things about showjumping is that it simply isn't possible to look at a group of horses and, going by conformation alone, pick out the ones that will be good jumpers: there have been beautifully put together animals which still have not been able to do all the right things, whilst others that have been freaks in appearance, have gone from success to success.

If, however, you are considering buying a horse with a view to jumping it, it is definitely worth looking for one that has reasonably correct conformation (unless it already has a proven track record in competition, in which case you might be prepared to overlook certain defects). Good conformation will not only make a horse easier to ride and train, but if, ultimately, it just isn't going to make the grade as a jumper at the level you want to compete at, it will be far easier to sell on or to change to a different sort of work, such as dressage or hunting.

Good conformation is not so much about beauty as practicality where jumping is concerned; a great deal of stress and strain is imposed on a horse that competes regularly – even at local level – and if it is well put together it is more likely to withstand it and stay sound. While there are no set rules about what will make a good jumper, there are certain characteristics which will make the horse's job that bit easier; and the more comfortably it can cope with its job, the more co-operative and willing it will be, and the more likely it is to go further.

If, however, you possess a horse that does not quite conform in all respects to what is generally regarded to be the ideal make and shape, do not despair. If it has sufficient ability, and is careful and brave, it is possible for it to cope with the odd defect and get there in the end; some of the best horses in the world have had dreadful conformational faults! Do not forget, though, that while you can improve the physique to a certain extent with proper feeding and work, you cannot change the basic conformation. You must do the best you can with what you have, but bear in mind that you may occasionally have to make allowances for its shape when training, and accept that there may be some things which it will find physically difficult – or even impossible – to do. Without appreciating these points fully, you will find it difficult to get the best from your horse.

There are many very good books which deal with conformation in depth if you wish to go into the subject in more detail, but the main features to look for in a horse you wish to train for jumping are described here.

PROPORTIONS

Although the horse may have many good points when they are assessed

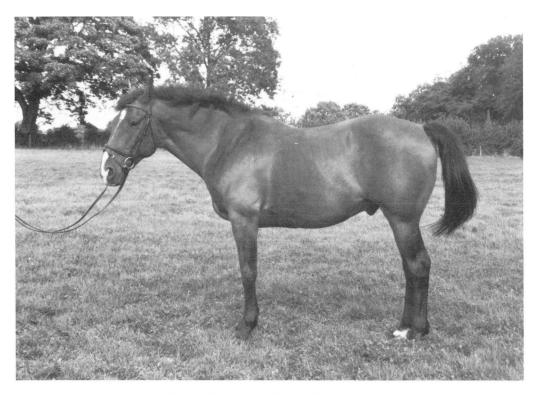

This gelding is a little upright in his shoulder, short of length of rein, and rather overtopped; in his favour, however, he is short-coupled and has a lovely backside! Try to look for positive points as well as negative ones and bear in mind that sometimes a horse can prove to be a talented jumper even though its conformation may not be ideal. If a horse has ability, and you can appreciate the problems that make and shape may present for it, you will be able to help it realize its potential fully.

individually, do try to get an overall impression of whether they fit together harmoniously and in proportion generally. For example, the head should not be too large and that the legs should not be too short in relation to the frame as this can affect balance, length of stride and freedom of movement, making it difficult for him to use himself efficiently and in a co-ordinated manner.

Head and Neck

The horse's face is often one of the first things you notice. A large, generous eye, pricked ears and a kind expression usually indicate an alert, outgoing horse with an honest and generous nature. While these qualities are not necessarily any indication of its potential ability, it will certainly make training and caring for it much easier and pleasanter, and its performance and progress is likely to be much quicker and more consistent than

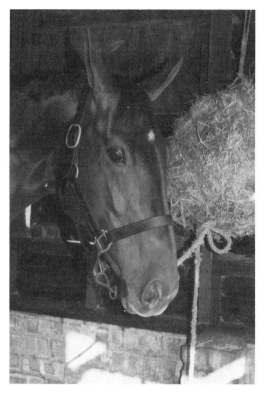

If the horse is very thick through the jowl – this is often accompanied by a short, stocky neck – it will be difficult for it to accept the bit and adopt a better outline. In this instance, you simply have to do the best you can, but there is no point in trying to force it to do something it physically cannot manage; it will only result in its becoming resistant through the jaw and in the muscles on the underside of its neck. Persisting may lead to rearing, so do beware of creating more problems than you started with.

There are few successful ewe-necked jumpers so, if you are buying a horse, this is a feature to avoid; the horse will tend to be on its forehand and, with an incorrect, high head carriage to try to compensate for this, will produce a hollowed back and trailing hocks.

Shoulders

A good sloping shoulder allows free movement and is a better shock-absorber than a short, upright one; if a horse is a little cramped in this department it can find it difficult to snap up its front legs over a fence. Action and conformation are closely linked to each other: if the horse uses its shoulder freely in walk, it usually means that it will work well over a fence. The gaits will also be more fluent and comfortable, and the horse will be better able to lengthen stride when asked; a horse with an upright shoulder will tend to have a choppy stride and will often find lengthening difficult, so it is best with this type not to ask for too much until it is more elastic and supple otherwise it is likely to rush and become unbalanced, propping its weight on to the forehand. Although this sort of horse is rarely an elegant jumper, it is often

While the horse's expression is no guide to its ability, it is a good indicator of its temperament and general attitude to life. Obviously it will be far easier to train and 'click' with one that has a nice character. This horse has a lovely eye and is alert and interested in the camera pointing at him and his surroundings in general. He also has big ears, which often seem to accompany a good temperament.

with a grudging or nervous personality. It should never be forgotten that being able to form a good relationship is vital; successful jumping at any level is, after all, a partnership, and it is much easier to 'click' with a horse that is easy to get on with.

How the head is set on to the neck should also be taken into consideration.

very clever at getting itself out of trouble, able to find an extra half-stride before a fence when necessary.

One other benefit of a good shoulder and reasonable length of neck is that it will make you feel far more secure, which can go a long way towards increasing your confidence and as a result developing a more positive attitude. If your horse is a little narrow across the shoulders, which will also give you the feeling that there is 'not a lot in front' it can often help to fit the horse with a saddle that is wide across the waist and with more pronounced knee rolls to compensate for this (although obviously the flaps should not actually interfere with the shoulder movement).

Withers

If your horse has very high or pronounced withers it is very important to make sure that the saddle is a good fit. Although it may look fine when working on the flat, if the horse jumps very round, the front arch of the saddle may well catch the horse and will soon discourage it from making a good shape over fences. For comfort, there should be a minimum of three-fingers' breadth between the front arch and the withers when the rider is mounted.

Back and Loins

A long back often tends to lead into poor quarters trailing away behind, and it is more difficult for a horse that is built like this to engage its hocks correctly, so many people prefer to see a short back. Although it is generally easier to ride a short-backed animal and for it to bring its hocks beneath its body, it is possible for the back to be too short, leading to difficulties in saddle fitting. A saddle that is too long in the seat will interfere with the action of the loins, which, together with the quarters, form the 'powerhouse' that propels the horse forwards and upwards. With short-backed horses it is often necessary to use shorter-seated saddles, but this can make it difficult for the rider to adopt a good, balanced position in the air. A short-backed horse is also far more likely to over-reach.

Although there are many good long- and short-backed horses around, the former may have more problems tackling uprights, and the latter be less scopey over wide-spread fences. Both will need to be ridden accurately at these types of fence.

Limbs

Good limbs are important on a jumper since they are not only responsible for propelling the horse forwards and upwards (in the case of the hind legs), but for the support of the full weight of both horse and rider on landing after a fence (in the case of the fore legs). A strong forearm is an asset as it is able to come right up and pull the shoulders forward over a fence so that the legs can be tucked up tightly; short cannons are also preferable as there will be less strain on the tendons, whilst good angles in the pasterns and shoulders all help to reduce jarring.

Short, upright pasterns (often associated with an upright shoulder) will be strong, but suffer more from the effects of jarring and concussion. However, overlong or very sloping pasterns can be just as much of a problem: they are better at shock absorption, but cause a

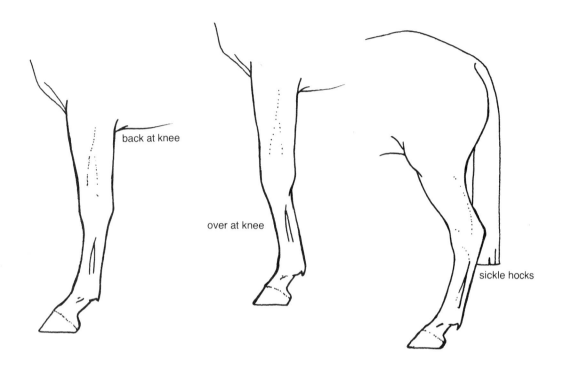

Conformational defects to avoid.

lot of strain to be placed on the tendons, and the bottom of the fetlock joint may even suffer cuts from the ground as the horse's weight is suspended over it on landing.

Calf knees also make for poor shock absorption and there may be restricted extension of the forelimb action. Poor foot conformation, such as contracted heels, boxy feet, and flat soles, also tend to suffer more from the effects of concussion and may ultimately lead to soundness problems. As regards the hind limbs, when the horse is standing still he should do so with his hocks well underneath him, giving an impression of power, rather than trailing out behind him. However, 'curby' or 'sickle' hocks are not ideal, as they can give rise to excessive strain on both the joint itself and the tendons below.

Obviously if the conformation is poor there is not a lot you can do about it other than encourage your horse to carry itself in as efficient and balanced a way as possible so that the risk of strain or injury arising as a result of poor make-up is reduced to a minimum. By recognizing potential weaknesses in conformation, you can do a lot to avoid future problems; it will also help you to understand why your horse jumps in the way it does, and to decide how much it can be changed without asking the impossible.

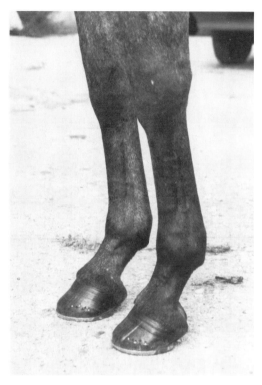

Good feet are an asset. This mare has a very turned-in near forefoot which imposes uneven stress on the joints, although ironically this particular individual has never suffered a day's lameness in her life! However, if you are buying a horse you could be taking a gamble as it is potentially a weakness.

SIZE AND TYPE

Size and type can be as important as conformation, and choice will be governed to an extent by the height and weight of the rider. On the whole, smaller horses are easier to ride: those with an infusion of pony blood often prove to be clever, quick-witted jumpers, nimble on their feet and better able to extricate themselves from difficult situations. A smaller horse often makes faster progress in his training and, provided he is well proportioned and the conformation is reasonable, is also more likely to stay sound.

One of the most common traps riders fall into is in overmounting themselves, feeling that they ride better, are more secure, and look better on a big horse. This is rarely the case and all too often a small rider on a large horse may not have enough control or strength to ride it properly. Such a situation is safe for neither horse nor rider, and inevitably leads to the horse becoming disobedient and all too aware of its advantage over the rider, who may well resort to adopting a poor position in order to try to cope. Big horses generally tend to mature later and are less well co-ordinated, more difficult to ride into an outline, and lack the athleticism of a smaller horse, requiring more flatwork initially. In most cases, a 15.3hh horse can usually do everything an amateur rider wants (some of the best Grand Prix horses have been under 16hh).

Type can also have a bearing on how much you can expect. For example, a cobby horse is unlikely to have the scope to jump bigger tracks and will need to be more accurately ridden to spread fences, which does not mean to say that you cannot have a lot of fun and enjoy a certain amount of success if the horse has sufficient flair and enthusiasm for the job. At the opposite extreme from the more stuffy cob types are Thoroughbreds, and thoroughbred and Arab crosses, which are often more sensitive and highly strung, requiring tactful riding and plenty of patience. Trying to bully or be very dominant with these types rarely succeeds and you should certainly

This mare is a little long in her back and also looks a little weak through her quarters and hind legs, which could prove a problem as this is where the main propulsive thrust is generated. Her rider is also a little over-horsed, and although big horses may not necessarily become very strong they do need more riding together which is not always easy for smaller riders. One other point about this picture is the horse's expression: she looks totally fed up with life, which perhaps does not bode well!

take this into account when buying a horse: either choose one whose temperament suits your attitude and style of riding or be prepared to adapt yourself to fit in with the horse's requirements. Of course, having said that, there are always exceptions to the rule; all horses are individuals and although it is possible to

Whatever the size and type of horse, one rule is common to them all: before starting gymnastic work make sure your horse is fit enough, as it can be very demanding. Neither should the horse be carrying too much excess condition as, especially when under stress or on hard ground, it will put an unnecessary strain on heart, wind and limbs.

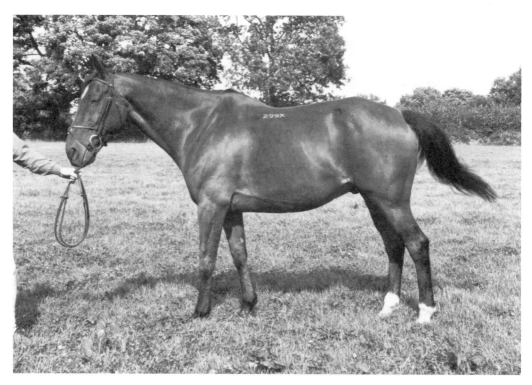

Darcy is certainly no oil painting to look at, but as can be seen from the photograph of him jumping (below) he nevertheless has great enthusiasm for his job and tries very hard for his rider, so that they are both able to have a lot of fun competing at unaffiliated shows throughout the year. Although he is never going to make a Grade A showjumper, his temperament, willingness and attitude mean that his rider gets a lot of satisfaction and enjoyment in training him to be successful – despite his conformation – at a less exalted level.

generalize, you cannot expect each and every one to fit neatly into a particular compartment.

TEMPERAMENT

Temperament is perhaps more important than anything else. In theory, any horse can jump a fence, regardless of the horse's size, shape or quality (although in theory designer-bred horses with good conformation should be able to jump bigger and better), but in practice, a horse's ability also depends on its temperament and how much it uses its brains. A positive-thinking horse will go forward and tackle its fences at whatever stage of education it is at; one with a negative outlook will not, and is less likely to help itself or its rider. Schooling can help develop respect and discipline in more wilful animals, but the work must always be kept varied and fun – especially with a sourer animal who may benefit more from being schooled whilst out hacking than at home all the time. Obviously a good temperament to start with is an asset. A placid, generous, intelligent and level-headed horse with an easy-going nature is the ideal, whereas those which are very sharp and buzzy can be very difficult to ride fluently to fences, and sometimes the brain can end up overtaking the body and legs, causing poles to fall unnecessarily. Boldness is also a good quality, but in all fairness, a spooky horse which takes a good look often makes a better jumper at the end of the day because it does tend to be more careful and does not get itself into trouble.

If you do not have a horse with the ideal temperament, it does not necessarily mean that you are not going to be successful with it, but you will probably need to be far more careful about tailoring the work you do to suit it. Do not be afraid to experiment a little with feeding if need be (particularly with more lively types); a lot of people are guilty of overfeeding, and a combination of too many concentrates and too little exercise is one of the commonest causes of horses playing up and misbehaving. A regular, organized routine and sensible, firm and fair handling, plus the opportunity to get out in a field for a few hours a day to relax, can also do a great deal to develop a better attitude and frame of mind. The more contented and relaxed a horse is in its home environment, the easier it will be to handle and ride, and the quicker you will be able to make progress with it, so don't underestimate the value of attention to this sort of detail.

Unfortunately a lot of young horses – or even older ones – have their temperaments detrimentally affected by human beings. This can happen when a horse is allowed to misbehave without a suitable reprimand, and also when a horse is punished unfairly or excessively. If you do your best to treat your horse as though it is at primary school – being taught right from wrong at the very start – there will be no need for a lot of 'sorting out' later on, which can cause a lot of resentment. While you cannot change a horse's temperament as such, you can instil the right attitude in it if you go about it the right way. There are plenty of books around on equine psychology, and it is well worth consulting them to give you more feel for how a horse's mind works. Having a battle every time you ride is never a good solution to problems; the key lies in developing a good empathy with your horse so that you can decide on a correct course of action according to the situation, and ensuring that it enjoys its work so that it is more inclined to want to co-operate rather than rebel.

SEX

The matter of sex is a subject open to much dispute, and many riders have strong prejudices either for or against mares. Geldings have achieved a reputation for being generally more reliable and consistent, and mares for being unpredictable and temperamental, but this is not a rule which always holds true: there can be difficult geldings and good mares, and it is not really fair to praise or condemn one or the other merely on the strength of acquaintance with particular individuals you have known.

If you are going to generalize, you could say that geldings are often more forgiving and generous and will tolerate bad riding more readily, whilst mares can be more sensitive and touchy (particularly

This mare has a lovely length of rein but is very straight and upright in her shoulder. She also has a very long, sway back, which makes it difficult to jump comfortably and successfully. When jumping, she was not the most co-operative of horses, although she worked well on the flat and was excellent to handle and hack out. When you have this sort of situation, when neither the temperament nor the ability to jump are present, it is probably best to change to a different sphere of competition to which it is more suited. Whether the conformation is good or bad, the right attitude is vital if you are to have any success at all.

when in season), which is why they will sometimes go better for riders who are tactful and sensitive rather than very dominant. Mares can be very different when in season, and although careful riding and handling may be required at such times (as a general rule of thumb, ask a mare to do something rather than tell her) it should not be allowed to become an excuse for bad behaviour; quite often what is purely and simply disobedience is put down to 'mareishness' and unduly tolerated. On the plus side, mares do seem to possess more personality and the ability to look after themselves, and they often have an extra edge of sparkle that geldings may lack.

Both mares and geldings have their pros and cons, but whatever your personal feelings on the subject, try not to let it influence you too much; provided you enjoy riding a particular horse and it does its job well, its sex should not really make a great deal of difference.

3 Equipment

Riding is a high-risk activity, and especially so when jumping, so it is vital to use the right equipment for the job as far as saddlery and apparatus is concerned. In addition, all equipment should be well-cared for: your horse's tack should be kept clean and supple, not just for the sake of appearance, health and comfort, but because your life could depend upon it; rotten stitching and dry, cracked leather are a recipe for disaster. Whilst you may not always have the time to strip down and clean your tack properly every time you ride, try to find at least a few minutes to give it a quick wipe over as this is better than nothing, with a really thorough clean at least once a week, more often if possible. Regular attention is the only way to keep leather in good condition; once it has been allowed to suffer from neglect no amount of effort will be able to reverse the deterioration and restore it to its former condition. Tack cleaning is one of the best opportunities to check on the condition and safety of your saddlery so try not to skimp on it, even though it is not the most exciting of jobs.

Cotton and synthetics need proper attention too. Numnahs particularly should be washed regularly to remove the build-up of grease and dried sweat, and should also be given a quick brush over after use to get rid of loose hairs. Protective boots are often overlooked, but do not forget that the linings also need to be kept clean if dried sweat, dirt and loose hair are not to lead to soreness.

When buying new saddlery, always buy the best quality available. It may be more expensive initially but is a better investment because, with proper care and maintenance, it will be safer, last longer, and work out cheaper in the long term. There are quite enough risks as it is when jumping without adding to them unnecessarily by penny pinching.

Whatever you use must be correctly fitted. Whilst the tack you put on your horse will not make him jump bigger or better, and only good riding and preparation will improve his performance, nothing is more likely to create problems so quickly as badly fitting or uncomfortable saddlery and there really is no excuse for negligence.

BRIDLE

There are many very good and easily maintained synthetic bridles about, but certainly for jumping work at any rate, it is probably best to buy one made of leather. Leather is more likely to break in an emergency, whereas synthetics can have a very high breaking strain. Many people keep a working bridle for everyday use and a show bridle for competitions, but do make sure that an everyday bridle is in just as good condition as the smart one!

Nosebands

The simpler you can keep your saddlery

the better, but do not become too inflexible about this, as there is always a time and a place for adding to, or changing, your horse's equipment. Nosebands are a good example of this: in the most simple form, a cavesson noseband is basically just there for the sake of appearance or to attach a standing martingale to if necessary, but if you find yourself with a horse that tries to evade the action of the bit you may well find you have to try something different if you are to be in control.

With a horse that tries to evade the bit by opening its mouth, either a drop, flash, grakle or rope noseband will help (the latter should be fitted fairly firmly to be effective). A grakle is also helpful with a horse that tries to cross its jaws or put its tongue over the bit. Another noseband which can also be of use with this last problem, although rarely seen, is the Australian cheeker, which helps to keep the bit raised in the mouth; with stronger horses the central portion does also impose a certain amount of psychological restraint.

One other noseband worth mentioning

Flash noseband and Fulmer snaffle.

is the Kineton or Puckle, although its action does not aim at closing the mouth in order to establish or regain control; it can be quite successful with horses that

---

Rules for the Use of Nosebands

- A noseband will only do its job if it is fitted correctly. It should never interfere with the breathing and, when using grakles or dropped nosebands, make sure that the cheekpieces are not pulled across into the eyes.
- If your horse does try to evade the bit, before employing a different noseband, do check that the problem is not arising because of discomfort from the bit, rough hands or mouth problems such as sharp teeth.
- If the horse has a habit of putting its tongue over the bit, check that it is not because it is fitted too low in the first place.
- If you use a standing martingale, it should only ever be attached to a cavesson/rope noseband, or to the cavesson part of a flash noseband.

become strong and pull, but that tend to back off any form of bit that is more severe than a snaffle, as it places pressure on the front of the nose when the horse tries to resist. The tighter the noseband is buckled, the more severe its effect; it should only be used with a snaffle.

Reins

Reins can be bought in different widths, so choose a pair that you can hold comfortably; very wide reins can be a big fistful for a child while very narrow reins can cut into the fingers and be just as difficult to keep hold of for an adult. If you are using a bit requiring two pairs of reins, it does help to use reins of varying widths or different materials, so that you can easily distinguish between them without having to look down continually.

It is sensible to use reins that offer a decent grip, as plain leather can become very slippery when wet (either from rain or sweat). Rubber-covered or laced reins, web reins or plain leather/web reins with grips stitched on are ideal. Do make sure that reins are a sensible length, too (especially with children) as if they are over-long it is possible to get a foot caught through them when working with jumping-length stirrups.

BITS

There are no hard and fast rules where bitting is concerned, and whilst careful schooling can improve the way a horse goes and make him less resistant in the mouth, some horses can become very strong once they start jumping, so you must be prepared to try different bits if

A horse that is not comfortable in its mouth will never work well. With difficult horses the answer does not always lie in a stronger bit. In this picture it looks as though a drop, flash or Grakle noseband, and running or standing martingale might help. But more importantly still, the rider needs to become more secure and independent in her position so that she can ride him more correctly and sympathetically between hand and leg. At this instant, she is relying almost totally on the reins for control and her own support, and it is not surprising that as a result he is becoming more anxious and resistant in his mouth as well as moving in an unbalanced and unco-ordinated manner.

necessary. A stronger bit is not always the answer though; sometimes problems are caused by fear of the bit and more success will be found with something milder, so it can often be a case of trial and error to discover what produces the

Rules for the Use of Bits

- A horse will always try harder if he is comfortable, but it is important for the rider to be in charge, so try to strike a happy medium.
- Don't always blame the bit when things go wrong. A change may be advisable, but sometimes the rider is not entirely innocent in contributing to a problem.
- Make sure bits are the correct size and adjusted at the correct height in the mouth. Remember that jointed mouthpieces tend to hang lower than straight ones, and the bridle cheekpieces will therefore need to be adjusted when changing from one to the other.
- Every horse is an individual and needs to be considered as such – what works for one will not necessarily work for another.
- Do not use a stronger bit as a means of forcing a headcarriage.
- Reserve stronger bits for when you really need them rather than using them continuously, otherwise their influence may begin to wane. Swapping bits occasionally can also be a good idea with some horses.
- When deciding to use a bit, make sure that you fully understand its purpose and proper use. Very severe bits should not be used by inexperienced riders.
- If you are in any doubt seek the assistance of someone experienced to advise you.

best results. Buying a number of different bits in order to experiment can be expensive, so try asking your local saddler if you can 'hire' a bit for a few days to try it out before buying; many do offer this service now.

Resorting to a more severe bit is often frowned upon, and certainly you should not assume that it will provide the answer to all your problems, but it is a fact that no matter how much work you do, not every horse will go well in a traditional snaffle. The mouth is one of the most sensitive parts of the horse's body, and while it is true that a mistake in your choice of bit can undo a lot of hard work and destroy confidence, it is

equally possible to do a lot of damage with a very mild one. Having to haul hard and often at a horse's mouth in order to control it in a mild bit is just another way of bruising and frightening it and, providing you do not abuse it, opting for something more severe, but which the horse has more respect for, may prove to be kinder if it means you need to pull less, as well as being safer for both of you.

Factors Influencing the Bit's Action

When choosing a different bit, it should be borne in mind that there are factors other than type which will influence the comfort and severity of the bit's action.

Diameter of Mouthpiece

A wider diameter spreads pressure over the bars, so it is generally milder, but it can be uncomfortable for a horse with a short, small mouth. A thinner mouthpiece applies a more concentrated pressure, which the horse may have more respect for.

Width of Mouthpiece

This must be correct both for comfort and to prevent evasions. If the width is insufficient it will pinch the corners of the mouth, but if it is too wide the bit will slide across the jaw to one side causing discomfort and an uneven action. In the case of jointed mouthpieces, there will also be room for the tongue to be drawn back and placed over the bit, while the nutcracker action will be increased considerably; the joint may also rise up into the roof of the mouth when a contact is taken on the reins.

Material

Metal mouthpieces are the hardest, most durable, and most severe. Some horses simply do not like the feel of metal and may go more kindly in rubber-covered, vulcanite or synthetic mouthpieces. Copper mouthpieces are also sometimes used to encourage better salivation if the horse has a rather 'dry' mouth since this problem leads to increased friction and consequent soreness from the bit.

Cheek-Rings and Shanks

Eggbutt and D-shaped rings are more fixed and concentrate the action of the bit, while loose rings allow more play and will encourage the horse to relax its jaw. The larger the size of the rings, the less danger there will be of their being pulled through the mouth; bits with long cheeks such as Fulmer snaffles will also help to prevent this. The length of the shanks of curb-action bits, such as the Pelham, also has an effect on the severity of the bit; the longer the shanks the more severe the action.

Joints

A joint in the mouthpiece creates a nutcracker effect with increased pressure on the bars and corners of the mouth. If an extra link is incorporated, as in a French link, it helps to reduce the nutcracker action.

Twisted Mouthpiece

The twists produce a more severe action than a smooth bit, by digging into the tongue, bars and corners of the mouth.

Ports

A raised central section allows a little extra room for the tongue, and has a more direct effect on the bars as a result.

Rollers

The movement of the mouthpiece helps to encourage salivation and prevent the horse from grabbing hold of the bit; cherry rollers are larger, rounder in shape, and milder.

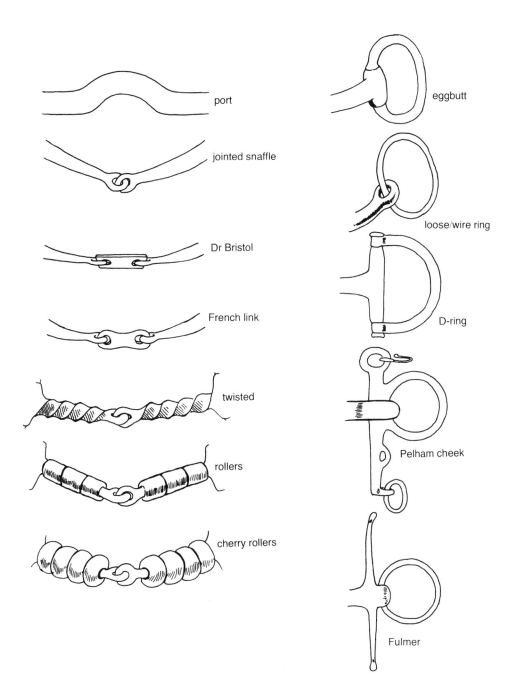

Cheek and mouthpieces of bits: (left) port, jointed snaffle, Dr Bristol, French link, twisted, rollers, cherry rollers: (right) eggbutt, loose/wire ring, D-ring, Pelham cheek, Fulmer.

Types of Bit

Although it may seem that there are many thousands of different bits, most of them are just variations of a couple of main types; you will probably come across many other variations than those listed here, which is just a brief guide to the most popular jumping bits.

Snaffles

The snaffle is probably the most popular of all the bit families, of which the jointed snaffle is the most commonly

Flash noseband and four-ring snaffle. This bit is known by more than one name – Continental snaffle, Duo, Dutch gag – so take care if you are ordering one!

seen. A useful variation with a young horse is the Fulmer, which has long cheeks that help to 'push' the head around when riding turns and circles, as well as preventing the bit from being pulled through the mouth. When used with leather keepers from top cheekpiece to bridle cheekpiece the full benefit is gained, but the action does become more fixed.

Still mild in action is the French link, which has a small extra link in the central joint, helping to create a more relaxed jaw. This is not to be confused with the Dr Bristol, which is similar in appearance but harsher in action and useful with a strong horse. The central plate is longer, with straight edges, and hangs at a slight angle to the rest of the mouthpiece, increasing pressure on the tongue.

The Continental or four-ring snaffle, as it is variously known, is very popular nowadays, but when the reins are attached to the lowest ring, it can be very severe. It is a good idea to use two pairs of reins with this bit, one attached to the snaffle ring, and the other to one of the lower rings so that you have the option of a milder or severer action according to how the horse is going.

Gag Snaffles These vary from conventional snaffles in that the top and bottom of the bit's cheekpieces have slots pierced in them through which a length of cord or rolled leather passes. One end is attached to the bridle headpiece and the other to the reins. As a firmer contact is taken on the reins, the bit slides up the cord or rolled leather and a strong pressure is applied to the poll and corners of the mouth; the larger the ring, the greater the leverage. In the right hands, the strong raising effect can make it a

Rope noseband and American gag snaffle.

(one pair attached to the snaffle section) so that the gag action is not continually in use, but only when needed, otherwise the mouth can become deadened and lacking in sensitivity.

Pelhams

This family of bits tries to combine the action of a snaffle with that of a curb within one mouthpiece. Pelhams can be used with either two pairs of reins or, if you are not very confident of your ability to cope with them, with one pair of reins attached to leather couplings or roundings. Kimblewicks are generally used with just one pair of reins; both use a curb chain, which is less likely to slip up the jaw on the latter than the former. A lip strap should therefore be used with a Pelham to help prevent this from happening. With a Kimblewick, the position of your hands will affect the amount of curb action – less when they are higher, and more when they are lower.

Bitless Bridles

Although this is not a bit, it is an alternative to using one. Occasionally you will find that a horse will not go kindly in a bit for some reason and a bitless bridle is the only answer. It should be stressed, however, that it is nevertheless very severe in its action and does need to be used with the utmost care by the rider. The longer the shanks, the more severe the effect and the greater the amount of tact required by the rider. Care always needs to be taken when fitting bitless bridles to ensure that they are positioned well above the ending of the nasal cartilages so they do not interfere with breathing, and that the front is well padded,

successful bit with a horse that leans hard against the bit and bears down on the rider's hands; a curb-type bit is not always very successful in dealing with this sort of problem as it often results in the horse becoming overbent and very heavy in front.

The American gag is a variation on the above and, like the four-ring snaffle, it has achieved a certain amount of popularity. The curved, sliding, metal cheekpieces exert a similar action to the gag snaffle, but with a strong action on the poll and a more limited amount of upward movement available in the mouthpiece. With both these bits, it is a good idea to employ two pairs of reins

Blairs pattern hackamore. This is fitted slightly on the low side. Always take care that it does not interfere with the breathing.

since a snug fit is needed and otherwise chafing will occur. Change the height slightly from time to time so that callouses do not form.

MARTINGALES

The action of running and standing martingales is preventive rather than corrective, the aim being to prevent the horse from raising its head so high that it can evade the rider's hand. This item of saddlery is all too often abused. If your horse needs a martingale, by all means use one, but do make sure it is correctly fitted so that it comes into action only when your horse lifts its head above the point of control; it should never be so tightly adjusted that it interferes with the action of the reins or restricts the horse in the head and neck when jumping. If it is too tight it will also affect the action of the bit, pulling it on to the bars of the mouth and causing bruising. A standing martingale is most effective when used in conjunction with a rope noseband.

One other martingale which can be useful when dealing with a horse that not

---

Rules for the Use of Martingales

- Never attach a standing martingale to anything other than a cavesson type noseband, or the cavesson part of a flash noseband.
- When using a running martingale, make sure rubber rein-stops are fitted to prevent the rings from running down and becoming caught in the bit. Although some reins do have leather stops stitched on already when you buy them, these do become a little floppy and ineffective with time.
- Make sure that a rubber stop is fitted at the intersection of the neck- and breast-straps, otherwise the breast-strap will droop down in a loop and can become entangled with the front legs.

only raises its head too high, but becomes very strong, is the Market Harborough. This is similar to a running martingale, but differs in that the straps, which normally slip over the reins, instead pass through the bit rings and clip onto metal D-rings stitched on to the reins. As with running and standing martingales, it should not come into action when the horse is working correctly, only when the head is raised too high.

SADDLES

Your saddle needs to be a really good fit if your horse is going to give of its best; at the same time it also needs to allow you to sit correctly and effectively. A specialist jumping saddle is the ideal, but if you can only afford one saddle, which has to be adaptable to allow you to participate in other activities as well, a general-purpose saddle is a reasonable compromise. Beware those that have flaps cut slightly on the straight side, or with a very short seat, as this will make it difficult for you to follow the horse over a fence in a good, independent and balanced position.

Decent knee-rolls are an asset and will give a feeling of security. When the saddle is fitted to the horse, check that the seat is level and not sloping backwards as this will tip you forwards into a collapsed, weak position; at the same time, it will concentrate pressure on the horse's back towards the rear of the saddle, instead of spreading the rider's weight more evenly over the muscles along the length of the seat. In time this will cause considerable tenderness and the horse will work in a hollow outline. When buying a saddle

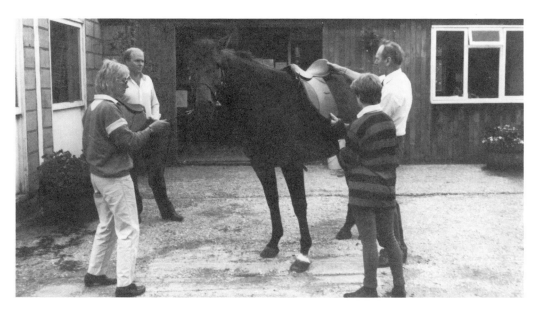

Asking a saddler to visit you with a selection of saddles can save a lot of time and energy when buying a new one.

with more forward-cut flaps, check that they do not interfere with the movement of the horse's shoulders – particularly if the shoulders are rather upright – or end up pushing the seat of the saddle too far back.

It is not always easy to find a saddle that is a good fit for both horse and rider, so it can be a good idea to ask a saddler to visit you with a whole selection of different saddles which you can try. This will save an awful lot of trips back and forth to the shop. It is worth paying attention to finding the best possible saddle because, although it may not make either you or your horse better at jumping, it will certainly make the job easier, more pleasant and safer for you.

Girths

There are many good quality girths available, ranging from the synthetic ones, which are tough, easy to maintain and soft on the horse's skin, to the leather ones, which need more care but look smart. Lampwick and web girths are best avoided as they are notorious for snapping unexpectedly, and mid-flight over a fence is not the best time to discover this for yourself. A jumping girth much in vogue is the Atherstone stretch, which incorporates a section of strong elastic which allows a certain amount of expansion with the horse's movements over a fence. When tightening the girth, always do it on the elasticated side, and do keep an eye on it, as the elastic will become tired and weak, losing its stretchiness with time and use, and will need to be replaced.

Using an overgirth as well is a sensible enough precaution to take because, no matter how careful you are with your saddlery, it is not unknown for a girth-strap to break or for the web to come adrift, and an overgirth will at least give you the chance to pull up and sort everything out without both you and the saddle parting company with the horse. If you use an elasticated girth, you should always use an overgirth.

Unless you have keepers on the saddle flaps for this purpose, use a breastplate, which you can thread the overgirth through, beneath the horse's chest, so that it cannot become displaced and end up sliding backwards to become a bucking strap.

Irons and Leathers

Sound stirrup-leathers are obviously an important part of your equipment, and those made of buffalo hide are ideal for jumping; they do stretch quite a lot, and may need new holes punched in them, but are virtually unbreakable. Whatever your leathers are made of, they will stretch to a certain extent, often slightly unevenly; swap them over once a week to keep the stretching as equal as possible, otherwise it can lead to your riding crookedly, both on the flat and over fences, causing problems.

Fairly heavy irons are a great help as they will not swing around so much if you accidentally lose one, making it easier for you to regain it. They should be the right size for your feet, with a clearance of about 1.2cm (½in) on either side of the widest part of your foot. Too small or too large a stirrup iron is asking for trouble, as your feet can easily become wedged or slip right through.

Rubber treads will help to prevent your feet from slipping in the irons, especially when riding in wet conditions or with leather-soled boots; but never tie your feet to the irons, or the irons to the girth, as it is absolutely essential that in an emergency you can kick your feet free, and that the leathers can become detached from the saddle.

BREASTPLATES

If the saddle fits well you should not need a breastplate; however, if you have a horse with poor conformation or a horse that is very fit, the saddle may slip backwards a little when jumping, and a breastplate will help it to stay in the right place. You should also use a breastplate if using an elasticated girth as the saddle will be more likely to slip.

NUMNAHS

A numnah or saddlecloth will help to protect the saddle from damage caused by dirt and sweat, but it must be kept clean. A thicker 'jelly' numnah can be handy if you have a horse that is a little cold-backed, and it does provide a certain amount of cushioning; but it should never be used to make a saddle fit or to excuse poor riding. Numnahs and saddlecloths must be pulled well up into the front arch of the saddle otherwise they will press down on the spine and cause soreness, and there is no point in going to all the bother of getting a saddle to fit correctly if you are going to undo it all.

BOOTS AND BANDAGES

Prevention is better than cure, so protective boots are a must. If your horse injures itself through lack of protection it can bring a halt to your work with it until it recovers – and a bad knock can also cause a crisis in confidence.

Brushing boots with velcro fastenings are quick and easy to put on, but the straps do need to be kept clean if they are to adhere properly, and it is wise anyway to take the added precaution of taping over them with insulating tape, just in case one does go astray; a boot that has slipped down can very easily bring a horse down.

Do provide some kind of leg protection as injuries can happen all too easily and may involve lengthy lay-offs. Some horses are more careful after they touch a pole, in which case use open-fronted tendon boots.

If your horse's technique in front is not the best in the world, but it tends to be more careful if it does touch a pole, open-fronted tendon boots might be a better bet on the front legs; some horses can be much like children, who, having touched a hot kettle and found that it hurts, won't do it again – it is a case of knowing your horse. Fetlock boots are another alternative, but only offer protection against the horse brushing low down; tendon boots have an advantage in that the reinforced rear section does offer good protection to the backs of the front legs (it is very easy for the horse to strike into the front tendons with the toe of a back foot when jumping).

Exercise bandages, if correctly applied, can help to lessen vibrations passing up the legs during work, but if used instead of boots they need to be expertly put on to be of any benefit; poor bandaging can in fact lead to tendon damage. To be really secure, they should also be taped or stitched into place, all of which can be very time consuming. A common myth is that bandages and tendon boots support the tendons; they don't – they only protect them from direct injury.

All boots must fit properly, and over-reach boots no less so. It is easy for the horse to strike into itself, so these provide protection for the heel region. However, they should not be so long that the horse can actually stand on the backs and trip itself up; if necessary, trim the edges with a pair of scissors.

STUD-GUARD

If you use studs, use a stud-guard. Even if your horse does not have a generous knee action, it is something you are

A stud-guard protects against injuries from studs or the heels of the shoes. This one has been lined with Fybagee to make it more comfortable.

trying to promote through gridwork and if the horse punctures or bruises its chest with the studs or heels of its shoes, it will hardly be keen to repeat the performance.

DRAW REINS

Of all the schooling gadgets, draw reins are probably the most frequently used – and abused – and the most controversial. It can be frustrating when things are not going right and, at some stage, there is almost always going to be a certain amount of temptation to resort to some kind of schooling gadget, especially when so many top riders are seen using them and getting good results with their horses. While there can be a time and a place for draw reins – in the case of an older horse who is very strong and set in his ways, for example – it is important to realize that getting the best out of them does require very skilful riding if they are not to create more problems than they solve.

An example of this is the commonly heard complaint that things are fine until they are taken off, when the horse reverts, its head coming up and resisting the bit. Draw reins literally pull the horse's head towards its chest (the leverage which can be exerted is considerable) making him overbend. When working in such an exaggerated outline, a lot of leg is needed to engage the quarters properly, otherwise the horse ends up pulling with its shoulders instead of pushing from behind, very heavy on its forehand and fixed in a rigid outline, which is not the object of the exercise. Frequently, once the draw reins are removed, the horse ends up going just as badly, if not worse, than before they were used. Whilst it can be hard work to achieve a good outline, it is often possible with a little patience and effort to get there in the end if the horse is capable; it is probably more beneficial in the long term to invest in

---

Rules for the Use of Draw Reins

- Draw reins should only be used with a snaffle bit.
- If in doubt leave well alone and do not use them.
- Do get some advice and instruction from an experienced person when first using them.
- Always use a second rein attached to the bit so the horse becomes used to its action in combination with the leg. This will make the horse less likely to raise its head when the draw reins are removed.
- Do not ride with constant pressure on the draw reins, but mainly on the snaffle rein; only use draw reins when required, and then with a 'squeeze-and-ease' action so that the horse does not develop a fixed, rigid outline.
- When you can ride with the draw reins slack most of the time, do without them before either you or the horse starts to rely on them.
- Use a neck-strap to loop them through so there is less danger of a front leg becoming caught up in them.
- Do not jump in them as it is easy to restrict the horse.
- Do not ride for too long in them, as the horse will tire quickly and his back may become sore.
- Bear in mind that some horses are physically unable to work in an ideal outline, and trying to force the issue could lead to dangerous resistances, such as running backwards or rearing.

Getting the best out of draw reins does require skilful riding if they are not to create more problems than they solve. In this picture, although the horse appears at first glance to have a reasonable outline, a more careful examination reveals that it is running on to its forehand and is leaning against the bit. Although the rider is basically sitting in a good position, the hands are fixed and there is insufficient leg to bring the hocks properly beneath the horse. Better use of the leg, together with a more flexible contact, would create a better balance with the horse less on its forehand and less resistant to the action of the hand.

some good lessons with an experienced instructor to help solve the problems, than to spend a lot of money on expensive equipment which may not really be necessary, and which you cannot after all take into the ring with you when you are competing.

It is vital to remember that creating a good outline is not simply a matter of forcing the head into the 'right' position; it is concerned with overall elasticity, suppleness and co-ordination from jaw to hindquarters. A correct headcarriage is a reflection of these characteristics, and a measure of the lack of resistance to the rider's aids. Artificially forcing a certain headcarriage does not mean that acceptance of the hand or any of these other qualities will follow; in fact it is more likely to be the reverse. If, however, draw reins are really considered to be necessary, it is extremely important that they are used properly and with common sense.

THE RIDER'S KIT

There is no point in kitting out your horse correctly and neglecting yourself; obviously a hard hat meeting current BS standards and sensible footwear is a matter of common sense. A body protector is a good idea as it can help to reduce the level of injury sustained in the event of a fall; do not wear jewellery however, as it can result in nasty injuries in such circumstances. If you have pierced ears, small studs are acceptable, but dangling or hooped earrings can easily be pulled through the ear lobes; necklaces can become entangled, as can bracelets; and it is not unknown for rings to cause not just blisters, but to result in fingers becoming dislocated and even torn off in falls.

With a stronger horse, or in wet weather, gloves are an asset, giving a better grip on the reins, particularly if the latter are rubber covered and the gloves are of the sort which have rubber pimples on the palms.

Spurs are sometimes a great help if used correctly, particularly for riders with weak lower legs, or who are short in stature but riding larger horses and who need that little bit more help to get the horse going forward into the bridle.

Whatever saddlery you use at home, do check that it is permissable at shows. Bear in mind that the rulings of the various official bodies differ slightly from each other.

Carry a whip too; you can always drop it on the ground if necessary, but at least it is there if you need it. No matter how good a horse is, there is always an occasion when you may need a whip for a little persuasion, and you can guarantee it will be that one time you don't have it that you will most need it.

Get used to carrying the whip with equal facility in either hand, and practise changing it over so you can do so when needed efficiently and without dropping it or upsetting the horse. The whip should be used to reinforce aids, never as a punishment; use it just behind the girth so that it is associated with the leg aids, and if it is a short jumping whip, hold the reins in the other hand so that you do not catch the horse in the mouth. Although there may be the odd occasion when you may need to use it on the shoulder, most of the time this is not ideal as not only can it interfere with the rein contact but, being close to the horse's head, can also take the horse's attention back to the rider instead of forward to whatever is in front of it.

One final word about clothing, whether it be human or equine: what you use for schooling at home is one thing, but do check that it is correct for shows. Classes run under BSJA rules do have rules and regulations about this, and a great many unaffiliated shows do nowadays follow BSJA guidelines. Details of rules about permitted clothing and saddlery are to be found in the BSJA Rules and Year Book.

4 Preparation on the Flat

Your horse's flatwork does not need to be tremendously advanced in order for you to start doing some jumping, but before you can progress to more complex exercises and bigger fences you will need to obtain more control and accuracy. This aspect is something that is often neglected by amateur riders to the horse's detriment and can frequently lead to problems later on; if the horse is not supple, obedient and athletic on the flat, it certainly won't be over fences either, and it will never reach its full potential. Simply schooling over fences is not sufficient: although there may be some improvement it will be limited in extent and the horse will not always be consistent. This is where riders so often let their horses down and become disappointed and disillusioned, never achieving as much as they could.

The most difficult thing about jumping is not so much the fence itself, which is the horse's problem, but being able consistently to present the horse to each fence in a good balance and rhythm, with the right amount of impulsion and on a good stride so that it can make the most of its ability to jump high and clean. Time spent on improving the flatwork is therefore nothing but beneficial and should never be considered time wasted. Not only does it instill and develop these qualities, but also the habits of discipline and obedience. Jumping can often hype a horse up – especially more gassy types – and this is where good, thorough preparation really pays off; if you have

established discipline and respect on the flat you will have something to fall back on if your horse does become unruly or cheeky. The successful horse is the one who will go where it is pointed, stop, turn, and move with balance, rhythm and impulsion when it is asked. Apart from any other considerations, the horse will also be considerably less tiring and more enjoyable to ride. By paying attention to these details you will be able to avoid a lot of problems in the future.

Spending some time working on the flat is also a vital part of the process of forming a good relationship with the horse and discovering more about its personality, temperament, strengths and weaknesses, all of which can help reveal clues about how best to develop its jumping performance; developing a 'feel' for the horse's moods and how it is moving is as essential a requirement for getting the best out of it over fences as any specific jumping exercise you might devise.

Having said that, you do need to take care not to overdo things, which runs the risk of boring your horse silly. Although there may be occasions when you need to work a little longer in order to get the message across and achieve what you wanted, it does not pay to work a horse to the point of exhaustion or rebellion; you need to possess the good sense and judgement not to push it over the top and to know when to call it a day – a sentiment which applies just as much to jumping work.

If you have a problem it is best to

Start each work session in walk on a long rein to allow your horse a chance to loosen off before starting more serious work. It is also a good opportunity to correct your position. When riding never waste time that you could be using constructively.

avoid a major confrontation if possible; you may not win, and even if you do, the horse may be resentful. There is always another day, when coming to the work fresh and with perhaps a better, more positive attitude or more relaxed view of things, you will resolve it without too much fuss.

Little and often is a good guideline as to how much serious flatwork to do; quality is more important than quantity if you do not want to sicken the horse with it. How quickly and how well it progresses in its flatwork, as well as how long and how often to do it, depends

upon his age, conformation and temperament. If it is only four years old for example, it will be neither physically nor mentally mature enough to be able to cope with long periods of exertion and concentration, and twenty minutes of serious work a day may well be enough; asked for more the horse may run out of steam and enthusiasm and become soured by the demands made on it, which it is unable to meet. The same applies if a horse is not very fit, or is very stiff – far better to finish early on a good note.

Conformation will to a large extent

play a role in how much improvement you can gain through flatwork, and you may find it necessary to reach some kind of compromise. An example of this is a horse that is very thick through its jowl; it may as a result find it difficult to accept the bit and adopt a good outline. If this is the case, you just have to do the best that you can; but certainly there is no excuse for not teaching a horse to respect the hand and leg, and to be obedient generally. You should not overlook the value of hacking either as a means of increasing your horse's fitness and helping to keep it relaxed in its work; indeed, there is no reason why, with a little imagination, you cannot incorporate a few flatwork exercises into your hacks.

Do not be afraid of mixing flatwork and jumping exercises. With a horse that tends to switch off doing flatwork, popping over a small fence occasionally can actually be very beneficial, keeping it alert and interested. With gassier or unbalanced horses, doing a little flatwork between fences or grids will help to restore balance, discipline and concentration, and will establish a more workmanlike attitude.

Keep your work varied, and try not to

A little work without stirrups occasionally helps to develop a deeper and more independent seat; only with a good position can you be really effective. Do take care not to overdo it if your horse is unused to doing much work in sitting trot as it can make the back muscles sore and tender.

Flatwork – Basic Guidelines

- Avoid major confrontations.
- Don't overdo it: little and often is the rule.
- Ask only what can reasonably be demanded of a horse: take into account conformation, age, fitness and temperament.
- Keep the work varied.
- Work to a basic plan – but be flexible.
- Listen to your horse: forming a good relationship between you will make working together much easier and more productive.
- Be consistent.
- Know what you are aiming for, and keep your purpose in mind.
- Seek advice when you need it.

---

avoid doing those things that you find more difficult. It is often tempting to concentrate on those exercises you find easier and more satisfying, but you must keep your ultimate goal in mind. Try to have a basic plan to work to, although you should also be prepared to be flexible: you may plan to teach your horse a new exercise, but discover something else more urgently in need of attention, or it may just not be the right moment to ask for something. Always remember that it is better for your horse to co-operate and work with you, rather than against you. It often helps to ride a well-schooled horse as it usually gives you a clearer idea of just what you are trying to achieve with your own, as well as giving you a yardstick against which you can compare it. Theory is one thing, but there is no substitute for experiencing the real thing; if you are not sure how your horse should feel when going correctly then you will be working in the dark for much of the time.

There are many theories on the subject of schooling on the flat, but, for the sake of consistency and to give the horse confidence, try to use the same methods rather than chopping and changing, which can cause confusion. Having lessons with a good instructor whom you respect and whose ideas you believe in is probably one of the best investments you can make, and will go a long way towards helping you to avoid making mistakes which can be hard to put right.

OUTLINE

In order to jump consistently well and accurately, your horse needs to be light in front, with its hocks engaged well beneath it, and in order to achieve this you will need to try to work the horse into as good an 'outline' as its conformation allows. This is a phrase often used but not always properly understood. 'Outline' is basically the impression you gain of the horse when viewing him from the side. When working him in a correct

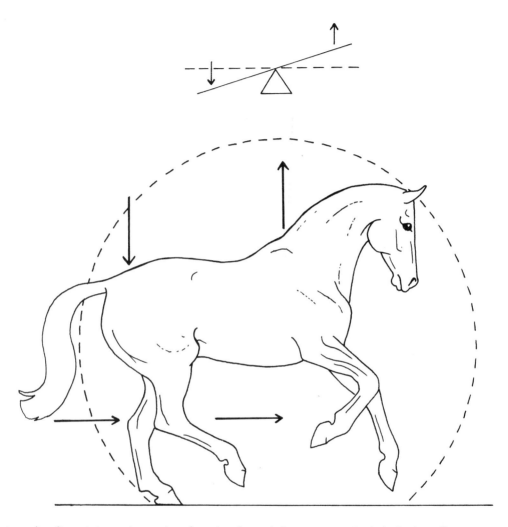

A good outline, giving an impression of a series of rounded, convex arcs. With the hocks well engaged beneath the body, the forehand becomes higher and more mobile – a little like a see-saw.

outline you should get a picture of a series of convex arcs blending one into another: longer, flatter curves with longer, free-moving strides in a youngster, or shorter, higher arcs with shorter, more elevated strides and increased engagement and lowering of the quarters in a more advanced horse. The showjumper is also asked to carry its face a little behind the vertical to really stretch all the muscles along the topline, but you should be careful when doing this not to fall into the trap of allowing the horse to drop behind the hand and leg, or to carry its head so low that its weight drops heavily on to the forehand. With its weight being mainly supported over its front legs, the horse is unable to use its hindquarters (the main propulsive force) properly, and even though it may be otherwise producing a pleasant, rounded outline, it is unlikely that it is using its back muscles correctly.

It is not enough to try to pull the horse into the correct shape by force alone; it is not a pleasant sight to see a horse being pulled in at the front end, or its mouth being sawed at, and it's unlikely that the horse finds it a pleasant experience either. Producing a good outline involves developing correct musculature along the top line, and this only comes with proper feeding and work over a period of time; there are no short cuts.

There are good reasons for trying to produce at least a reaonable outline. The horse which can do so will be able to work with maximum efficiency, strength, co-ordination, balance and staying power, both on the flat and over fences. The neck and jaw will be supple, accepting the rein contact; the hocks will be engaged well beneath it, supporting its body weight and lightening the forehand,

and the horse will be ready and able to do whatever the rider asks. By encouraging the horse to become more supple longitudinally through those muscles it will be asked to use when jumping, a good shape on the flat can be achieved, which will help the horse to adopt a good shape in the air, as well as making it possible for it to be in a good position to take the fence on.

On the other hand, the horse that tends to work on the flat in a 'hollow' outline (with concave arcs) will always be at a disadvantage, since it will tend to jump in a similar manner.

When beginning to ask the horse to work in a better outline, it is important to appreciate that you cannot transform it overnight – it has to be a gradual process. A horse's conformation will make it easier or more difficult, depending on whether it is naturally short and bouncy or long and rangy; but whatever its shape you cannot hurry the process over much and, although it may be hard work for both of you at first, it will become easier with time, patience, maturity and correct muscle

---

Hollow-backed horses will be:

- less efficient, needing to expend more mental and physical energy in order to do what is asked of them. For example, they will have to jump higher in order to clear a fence.
- more difficult to control.
- unable to increase or decrease speed so efficiently because they cannot engage their hocks properly beneath them.
- less well balanced.
- less safe to ride.
- more tiring and uncomfortable to ride.

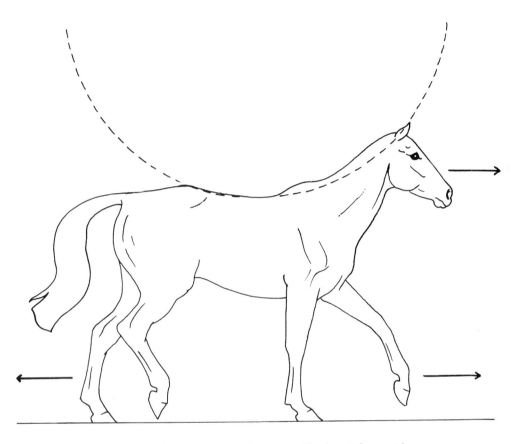

A poor outline and muscular development. A very obvious 'upside-down' shape with poor co-ordination and inefficient use of energy. The hind legs are not engaged beneath the horse and it is running forwards, propping its weight over its forehand.

development. Do not forget either, that if the horse is very stiff or unused to working in a correct outline, or has been allowed to get into bad habits and has developed incorrect musculature, it will not only find such work very demanding and tiring, but (if made to work like this for too long a time) it can become sore and tender in its back, and such discomfort leads rapidly to evasions. Allow periods of relaxation, allowing it to walk and stretch on a long rein, and taking

care not to overdo things until it finds it easier – it will be far more willing and co-operative for it.

When beginning each session, do allow your horse to start off walking on a long rein – although still with activity and a good rhythm – followed by a relaxed trot to allow it to stretch and loosen off before commencing more serious work. Some stiffer, older horses may also benefit from a short canter with the rider adopting a light seat; you will need to experiment a little to find out what suits your particular horse best. This warming-up phase can also be a good settling-in period for the rider, when you can concentrate a little on tidying up your position and loosening off your own stiffnesses, perhaps using a few exercises to help resolve them.

A point missed by many riders is that a correct outline involves the whole structure. When it moves in a good outline, the horse is well balanced, co-ordinated and united. All too often, riders become obsessed with pulling the horse's head in to create a semblance of an outline, although the horse may not have accepted the bit nor co-ordinated and engaged the quarters through the back muscles. A good, as opposed to a 'false', outline is created by several factors all coming together at the same time, of which the most important are probably that the horse accepts the rider's leg aids, accepts the bit, and moves with balance, impulsion and rhythm.

Accepting the Leg

One of the most common problems riders have is that the horse does not accept the contact of the leg. It either ignores it or, at the opposite extreme, runs from it. The horse must be obedient to the leg, stepping forwards (and if asked, sideways) in response to it; it must not be slow to react, otherwise you will never be able to create impulsion. Your legs must give positive, clear instructions: wriggling them about without being precise will be ineffective at best, confusing at worst. Try to avoid clamping your knees on to the saddle, as this will inhibit their action; instead turn them very slightly away from the flaps as this allows

the lower leg to achieve a closer contact with the horse's sides and to give aids that are more effective, sympathetic, co-ordinated and controlled. Gripping upwards and inwards is another very common fault, and while it may be largely ineffective on a lazy horse, it can have an electrifying effect on one that is more sensitive; along with the consequent problems of this, it also tends to weaken the position and, especially when jumping, can result in the rider ending up completely out of balance, particularly on landing. You should also try to make a conscious effort to use your legs independently of your body, as rocking the body or 'pushing' with your hands not only unbalances the horse, but can make his back very sore.

Because a shorter, jumping-length stirrup does tend to inhibit the movement of your legs to a certain extent, it is important that right from the very start your horse learns not just to respond immediately, but also to a fairly light aid; having to use a very strong leg all the time to keep the horse going is not only punishing on its sides, but, just as importantly, quickly leads to exhaustion in the rider – and a tired rider is more of a hindrance than a help.

With positive riding, the problem of a horse that does not respond quickly enough or to a light leg aid can usually be fairly quickly and easily remedied. Start off in walk, and with a soft aid ask your horse to trot. If he fails to respond, quickly give him a couple of sharp smacks with your stick just behind your leg, but make sure as you do so you have a light contact on the reins, as the horse is likely to shoot forwards quite rapidly and you do not want it to be restricted by contradictory aids which will make it resentful and confused. Give the horse a pat, quietly ask him to walk, and repeat the exercise again until you do get the response you want. Usually it does not take long for them to catch on. Do bear in mind that there can also be other reasons for apparent laziness, which might be worth investigating. The diet can be one cause of problems, so it is important to ensure that the horse is receiving enough of the right sort of feedstuffs for the work and exercise it is doing. Many feed companies employ their own nutritionists nowadays, and if you are in any doubt about this aspect of your horse's management, you can always ask them for advice. Another reason may be the horse's condition; if it is grossly overweight, or with a big bellyful of grass, it is hardly going to be fit for more athletic and demanding work, and it may be worthwhile keeping it stabled for part of the day, or else finding a barer paddock to turn it out in. Asking a horse to work hard while in such condition will not be good for its health anyway, as it will put a lot of strain on its limbs, wind and heart. Fitness is another factor, too, particularly if the horse starts off willingly enough, but runs out of steam after a while and starts to be slower to respond to your leg. It may not be that it is unwilling to respond, but that it is unable, and pushing a horse on when it has reached this stage can lead to injury and rebellion. It is not ideal, though, to get youngsters too fit before the habits of discipline and obedience are fully established, since if they do put up a fight for some reason you are unlikely to win – and it is essential not to find yourself in this situation.

At the opposite extreme is the horse that runs away from the leg, refusing to

Rosie is working quite pleasantly through this corner and accepting the bend well. It is by no means a perfect picture, though; she could be moving forward just a little more freely. This is probably caused in part by Nina's inside hand drawing backwards and downwards and becoming restrictive. With shorter reins her hands would be carried further forward and she would be more in tune with Rosie; she would have a far better feel of what she is doing and be more inclined to allow Rosie to travel forwards into the contact.

accept any contact from them at all, so that the rider often ends up with the leg pushed forwards and away from its sides and relying on the contact for control. This can lead to the horse becoming very short and tight in its neck, and with a resistant mouth; and since there is no leg to encourage the back end, it becomes stiff in its back, on its forehand and out of balance. Although it may take time to achieve, the horse must learn to accept and respond correctly to the rider's legs. Try to maintain a contact, albeit a very soft, even passive one to start with. Work in walk until you can achieve a constant leg contact and can begin to apply a gentle pressure; practising exercises such as turn on the forehand and leg yielding can also be beneficial. As this becomes more successful, so you can start to progress to some trot and canter work. With the naturally more gassy, uptight horse, care also needs to be taken with feeding, so as not to encourage it to become even more over the top. A good routine and good handling can do a lot to create a relaxed and contented horse, and this will be reflected in its attitude to work.

Impulsion

Impulsion is necessary at all times, but on your terms, not the horse's; if it is not totally relaxed and responsive to your aids on the flat, it certainly will not be when jumping one or more fences. There is sometimes confusion in the minds of riders as to the difference between impulsion and speed, which results in their pushing their horses out of balance, under the impression that if it is going fast (or even running away from the leg) then there must be plenty of impulsion. This is not necessarily true; speed can be defined as miles per hour, or the time it takes to cover a certain distance, whilst impulsion describes the manner in which the miles are covered: impulsion is contained, powerful energy used in a controlled fashion. The horse may cover the ground more slowly (as in collected gaits

with a shorter, more elevated stride) or faster (as in extended gaits with a longer stride), with balance and rhythm and with the hocks well engaged – in other words, with impulsion. Alternatively the horse may travel slowly and without activity and impulsion, or fast but with its hocks trailing, and with a hurried, irregular rhythm and poor balance; speed, or lack of it does not in itself imply the presence or absence of impulsion.

When trying to create impulsion, you should try to develop a feel for the horse's natural rhythm within each gait. Another very common fault is that of the rider, in his enthusiasm for getting the horse to go forward (particularly if it is stiff) to interfere with this natural rhythm and hurry the horse out of it. This can result in the horse running on to its forehand and either leaning on to the bit, or hollowing and raising its head in order to try to maintain some kind of balance.

Although initially you may be concerned with improving the work in walk and trot, take care not to neglect the canter work, as this is the gait from which you will eventually be doing a lot of your jumping, certainly in competitions. This is not to say that you need to spend long periods of time in canter. In fact, this can be detrimental if the horse is young or unfit, since it will tire quickly and may start to run on to its forehand. Ask for short periods of canter – a whole, or even half a circle perhaps – followed by a spell in trot or walk before asking for the canter again. The horse will learn nothing from being asked to canter for long periods in an unbalanced fashion, but provided you ride it correctly from the walk or trot into the gait, the transition itself can do as much to

---

Points to Remember When Asking for Impulsion

- Sit as correctly as you can so your aids are effective.
- If your horse ignores the leg aids, be prepared to reinforce them with your whip or spurs.
- Establish a regular rhythm in all gaits.
- Transitions to, from, and within gaits, are excellent for helping to engage the quarters better.
- Polework can also help considerably in encouraging more activity from behind.
- Sometimes working in canter can help a lazy horse to be more energetic.
- Work on circles is often beneficial, provided they are not too small for the horse to cope with; do make sure that your outside leg prevents the quarters from swinging outwards in order to avoid having to engage directly beneath the body weight.
- Increasing and decreasing the size of a circle is another useful exercise for helping to bring the horse's back legs further beneath him.

---

help get the horse light in front, balanced and working through from behind as anything else.

Some riders are confronted with problems caused by the horse's having too much impulsion, rather than a lack of it; this can happen either naturally, or because it has been ridden too strongly from the leg, or because it does not accept the contact and therefore the energy cannot be controlled. The first priority in this instance is to establish a very steady rhythm and a good-quality contact so that the impulsion can be regulated and contained. If the horse actually feels a bit lazy at first when doing this, do not worry; there is no point in creating more impulsion than you can control, or it will get the better of you and you will end up trying – unsuccessfully – to dominate the horse with your hands. As the contact improves and a better rhythm and

balance is obtained, it will be easy enough to begin gradually to restore more energy.

Half-halts

Half-halts are an invaluable rebalancing and reactivating aid, and you will gain far more from using them if you can think of them in this context rather than as merely 'checking' the horse and slowing it. They are applied in much the same way as when asking for a downwards transition, but with more subtlety so that they do not cause the horse to change down a gait, but rather abbreviate it. Your hand 'feels' the reins, followed immediately by a forward riding aid and a slight softening of the contact, which has the effect of retarding the forward movement and putting the horse's hocks beneath him again. This is useful with horses that tend to drop on to the

Half-halts are an invaluable aid to reactivating and rebalancing a horse. In this picture, Rosie has run on to her forehand and is giving every impression of going downhill. It is not helped by the fact that Nina has collapsed her ribcage, come behind the movement, allowed her reins to become too long and her lower leg to slip forwards, so that she is unable to push Rosie's hocks beneath her and ride her up into the bridle.

On the next circle, Nina has corrected her position considerably and ridden a couple of positive half-halts, resulting in a much-improved balance and more active canter – although she could still use a little more leg to good effect.

forehand or lean on to the rider's hands, as well as with horses that are inclined to be a little too onward bound and liable to put themselves out of balance. In most cases these problems arise because the horse is lacking in balance, rhythm and impulsion, and the half-halt, correctly ridden, helps to restore all three. Depending upon the level of schooling, you may need to use half-halts fairly frequently, but make sure they are brief, quick aids with only a momentary closing of the hand; do not get drawn into a contest of strength and resort to a continuous pull, as the horse will only start to lean against the bit.

Accepting the Bit

Achieving a good outline is largely a matter of achieving a good balance between your hands and legs. Having considered some of the other factors involved, this brings us on to the subject of rein contact and encouraging the horse to accept the bit.

A contact with the mouth from the rider's hands via the reins to the bit needs to be established in order to control the impulsion created by the rider's legs. This contact should be fairly firm, but with a certain elastic quality in the tension. Good hands are, it is said, the hallmark of good horsemanship, but it can be an elusive skill to acquire, especially when dealing with a stiff or difficult horse. It is a skill that requires much tact, sensitivity and patience, and a secure, balanced and supple position in the saddle so that the hands can act independently, rather than supporting the rider's body or compensating for weaknesses.

Although the signals through the reins should be positive, never make the mistake of holding the horse in a vice-like grip, or of irritating it and making its mouth sore by sawing from side to side with the reins. At the same time, a slack, loose rein is not a particularly sympathetic one either, especially if you are stiff in your arms and shoulders, because it usually results in jerky, snatching aids as well as allowing the impulsion to evaporate and be lost, with the horse running on to its forehand and becoming unbalanced.

When the horse is 'accepting the bit' it relates not just to the fact that it is salivating freely and yielding to the rider in its jaw and poll, but that it is doing so without showing resistance in any other part of its body either: it should still be moving freely forwards with springy, elastic steps, a swinging supple back, and moving without any appearance of woodenness or a stilted, choppy, forced action.

When trying to create this for yourself, it often helps to enlist some assistance from an experienced rider or instructor, as it is easy to develop nagging, fiddling hands or a somewhat fixed, rigid contact without being aware of it until problems have arisen. Having someone demonstrate on your horse and then talk you through the process is one way of learning how to achieve the correct contact. Alternatively, you may find it helpful to walk alongside your horse while it is being ridden, and holding each rein in turn between index finger and thumb, or to have your instructor stand in front of the horse in halt while you are mounted, holding both of the reins to illustrate the right amount of weight and elasticity in them.

Often the contact is very much firmer

Teaching a horse to accept the contact is not always easy, especially if you are inexperienced yourself and unsure of the 'feel' you are aiming for. Help from a good instructor, who can demonstrate it if necessary, is often a big help. The rider's footwear is worth commenting on: trainers are not ideal for riding in since the feet can slip through the irons and become trapped, but these particular trainers have been specifically designed for riding and are constructed with a proper heel.

than many riders anticipate, but provided you keep your leg on the horse to keep it moving forwards and prevent it from backing off the contact (but without hurrying its steps) and as long as your elbows, wrists, fingers and shoulders are supple, the contact will be flexible and not cause discomfort. Problems can and do arise, however, as already stated, if you are stiff or lacking independence in your seat, as this will cause you to rely on your reins for security.

Awareness of this, plus lunge lessons and trying to visualize your arms as an extension of the reins, will soon help to remedy this. Care does also need to be taken with maintaining a steady, rhythmical gait, as allowing it to become hurried will result in faster, shorter steps with the horse's weight being placed over its forehand. This frequently results in the horse's raising its head and neck, and hollowing in an effort to transfer weight backwards and regain its balance; in this

If you have problems achieving acceptance of hand and leg and a correct outline, be prepared to be a little patient. Maintain a contact with your legs, albeit softly if necessary, and a constant, elastic contact on the reins – neither slack nor rigid. In the first picture the mare is not really too enthusiastic about the idea, but the next picture shows a considerable improvement as her rider quietly but firmly perseveres. She could still be more relaxed but further softness will only be achieved with time and increased suppleness. Do not expect too much too soon, or imagine that you can miraculously transform a horse or solve all its problems within one work session. Incidentally, the numnah on this mare could be pulled further forward beneath the saddle; when it slides back like this it can actually interfere and be ticklish for the horse.

situation, it will certainly not be in a position to relax its jaw to your hand. Remember, it is activity you are after, not speed; slow down if you experience this sort of difficulty.

It is probably best to start off in walk as it is easier to prevent the horse from evading by using speed, and the rider is better able to maintain a balanced, independent and established position. Your hands should follow the movement of your horse's head, but without exaggeration or 'rowing' with them; you might find it easier to think of the motion of the horse's head moving your hands rather than trying consciously to follow it, which can lead to a jerky, inconsistent contact. Ask the horse to yield to the contact and soften through its poll and jaw with small, soft feels or squeezes on the reins, with supple fingers and wrists, and level, relaxed shoulders. If it resists, try to avoid pulling back and setting yourself against it; instead close your fingers in a restraining way, still with relaxed (not limp) arms, until it does soften. It does take time to achieve a consistent result, or even to obtain any result, so patience is vital!

As the horse does begin to relax its jaw to you, soften in return, but not to the point of throwing it away again. An easily made mistake is to give too much too soon, or else not at all, so that the rider either loses what he has achieved, never establishes it, or else creates a fixed jaw with the horse leaning against the bit. This is where the aid of a really good instructor helps, although a certain amount of trial and error is needed in order to gain experience and 'feel'; it does help initially if someone watching from the ground can suggest when and how much to 'squeeze' or 'ease'.

When asking the horse to accept the contact, easing the rein slightly is as important as squeezing. Easing the rein is the horse's reward for submission and discourages any desire to draw back from, or lean against, the bit; it also encourages it to carry itself rather than relying on the rider's hands for support. When it is accepting the bit correctly, the feeling should be of this elastic variation in the rein tension, with the impression that the horse has the confidence and desire to form a contact with the hand just as much as the hand forms a contact with the mouth. It should not be non-existent, with the horse drawing back from the bit, but with a certain amount of weight in the hand, although not to the point of making your shoulders ache. As a better 'feel' in the mouth and acceptance of the hand is developed, so more impulsion can gradually be created if required, with an improved outline and control.

Evasions

Sometimes problems arise when asking the horse to accept the bit, and it can often be tempting to resort to gadgets in order to achieve a result, but on the whole it is usually best to persevere and leave such artificial aids to the experts. When problems are experienced, it is often a good idea first to make sure there are no contributory factors which need remedying, such as discomfort from ill-fitting saddlery, rough hands, sharp teeth, lampas or mouth ulcers. You should also check that you are riding in balance and that your horse is not being ridden forwards too strongly and out of balance. The most common problems experienced by riders include:

Above the bit The head is carried high, with a concave, hollow outline, the nose poked forwards and upwards, trying to evade the contact; the horse may also be running forwards away from the leg and opening its mouth, attempting to put its tongue over the bit or crossing its jaws.

To correct this, try to establish a slower speed and correct acceptance of the legs, concentrating mainly on walk to start with. Check for physical problems and use a suitable noseband if necessary to prevent the horse from evading the action of the bit. Little or no contact will not teach it to accept the bit better, although excessive fiddling and nagging or a rigid contact should be avoided. Try to achieve an elastic tension and sustain a contact so it learns that it cannot avoid it; ask with the hands, then lighten them when it does yield to the bit. Lungeing in side-reins may also help, although side-reins should not be used to enforce a headcarriage.

Behind the bit This is when the horse tries to evade the contact by dropping behind it, drawing its face well behind the vertical and leaving the rider with little or no weight in his hands. The horse is often on its forehand, and the situation often arises because of a hand/leg imbalance – too much hand and insufficient leg.

To correct, use more leg to activate the quarters, thus lightening the forehand and pushing the horse back up into the contact; try to soften the contact a little, and be careful not to allow the horse to move forward too fast. Transitions and frequent half-halts will also help.

Leaning on the rider's hands The horse uses the rider's hands as a means of support, sometimes leaning very heavily; the horse is often very much on the forehand. Again, transitions and frequent half-halts are of great help, and the rider should take care not to encourage the habit by leaning on the reins or using them as support to compensate for a weak position. The horse needs to be asked to carry itself, rather than relying on the rider, so do not give it anything to lean on; keep the rein aids light and quick so it does not get the chance. Do not forget that you must use your legs to engage the quarters properly so the horse can become lighter in front, but avoid hurrying the steps as you do so.

Stiffness and physical problems Some horses find it difficult to accept the bit because of stiffness in the body; or because the conformation is poor (thick through the jowl, for example), or as a result of incorrect muscle development on the underside of the neck. Taking time to develop the correct musculature, lungeing in side-reins and using latecal movements, such as turns on the forehand and leg yielding, will help to supple the back and hips of the horse and make it easier for it to adopt as correct an outline as its build permits. It may also be worth having the horse checked out by a vet in case there are other physical problems which could be causing difficulties.

Teeth grinding This can sometimes be a habit, as weaving is, but it can occur because the horse is not truly accepting the leg and hand: it is in fact resisting the aids. Try to soften the contact, as the problem often arises from an unyielding hand trying to force an outline, and use lateral work to encourage a better overall acceptance of the aids. It often happens when the horse is upset or excited, when it is easy for the rider to react with tension, aggravating the problem; far better, if possible, to settle the horse into a walk again for a while and to let it relax.

LATERAL WORK

There are many school movements and exercises which can be employed to great benefit. It is important to keep work varied and interesting, as much for your sake as the horse's, since a bored rider will not produce any great enthusiasm for the job in the horse. At the same time, though, beware of trying to introduce too many new things at once, or you will run the risk of confusing and upsetting the horse. Establish each step properly before tackling the next one, which is not to say that your work needs to be boringly repetitive and predictable; it is a case of variations on a theme, rather than too many themes at once! Listing the exercises you could try would fill a whole volume in itself so there is not room for them in the space of one chapter, so it is well worth investing in a book on schooling exercises which could provide you with new ideas.

However, two exercises that are worth explaining here are the turn on the forehand and leg yielding. Both will help to develop increased suppleness and obedience to the leg, and neither requires the horse to be at an advanced level of work to introduce.

Turn on the forehand

This is the easiest movement of the two to start off teaching the horse because it does not require any change in balance or any degree of collection; provided the horse will accept a bend, it does not even have to be 'on the bit'. All that is required is that the horse is willing to stand still and accept the contact of hand and leg.

Basically, the hind legs perform a circle around the forehand, which remains at the centre of the turn. Initially, the steps with the hind legs may be slightly short, but as the horse becomes more supple and familiar with the exercise, so they will actually cross, the inside hind in front of the outside hind. Having established as square a halt as possible, the inside rein asks the horse to soften and bend inwards very slightly through the neck, while the outside rein prevents the horse from bending excessively to the inside and from walking forwards before the movement is completed.

The rider's inside leg then asks the quarters to move sideways away from the direction of the bend, while the outside leg remains in contact with the horse's side, but passively, until as many steps as are required are achieved, at which point it acts, together with the inside leg, to send the horse forwards again.

The practical benefits of the movement are that it teaches the horse to respond and yield to the action of a single leg, and promotes loosening of the quarters; it also teaches the rider better co-ordination of the aids. It is an exercise that you should use judiciously, however, as it does tend to place the horse's weight over its forehand and can lead to its becoming very heavy in front if practised to excess. You should take care when riding this movement not to draw your hands back or tip forwards as it can lead to the horse's learning to resist

Turn on the forehand.

by running backwards; at all times, try to maintain the feeling of the horse's being between hand and leg and with a desire to move forwards rather than backing off the contact. Another common pitfall is that of obtaining too much bend in the neck, so that the horse becomes unbalanced or learns to evade by drifting sideways with its shoulders; you should not be able to see more than the corner of its inside eye at all times.

It is usually best to teach this exercise with the horse away from the track, and initially to allow a little forward movement so as to discourage any desire to run backwards. If the horse is a little confused at first as to what is wanted of it, it can be useful to have an assistant on hand who can push the quarters around with a hand on the horse's hips.

Leg Yielding

As with the turn on the forehand, this movement is relatively easy to teach because it does not require collection, only a reasonable acceptance of the bit. The horse should already be familiar with the turn on the forehand, and comfortable in walk and trot through corners and on 16yd (15m) diameter circles before introducing it, when it should be performed in walk before starting to ride it in trot.

The horse should be bent very slightly away from the direction of movement, but do take care not to achieve too much bend in the neck, or the horse will evade by falling on to its outside shoulder. In this movement the horse is asked to move both forwards and sideways away

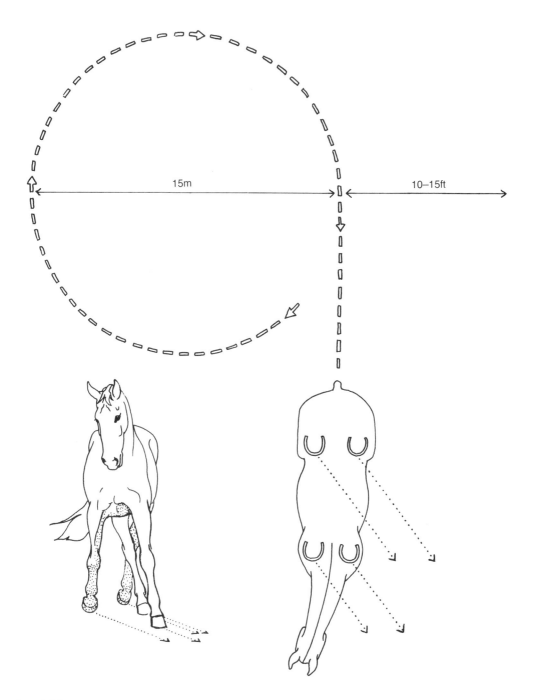

15m

10–15ft

Leg yielding.

from the pressure of the rider's inside leg, with both front and hind inside legs crossing in front of the outside legs. The rider's inside rein helps ask for and sustain an inside bend, while the outside rein prevents an excessive amount of bend, helps to prevent the shoulders from moving sideways in advance of the quarters, and controls the speed. The rider's inside leg asks for the sideways and forwards movement, whilst the outside leg maintains a close contact to prevent the horse from making too much sideways ground with insufficient forward momentum, and stops the quarters from swinging across in advance of the shoulders. This exercise encourages looseness and suppleness of the shoulders and hips, and teaches the horse to be more manoeuvrable and responsive to the rider's legs, as well as serving as an introduction to more advanced movements.

Probably the easiest way to introduce it is to work on a 15m (16yd) diameter circle at a distance of about 3–4.5m (10–15ft) away from the edge of your working area, making sure that both your legs maintain a good contact with the horse's sides, and that the horse is accepting a correct bend and moving with a steady, regular rhythm. Once you have established this, leave your circle at the point where it is closest to the edge of your working area, maintaining a slight bend still, and with an increased pressure of your inside leg ask the horse to step

forwards and sideways; the proximity of the edge of the working area will help to incline him to move towards it. Once he has grasped the idea, you can start to ride the movement in other places. When moving towards the edge of your working area, do try to keep the horse's body parallel through its length so that both shoulders and quarters travel across together, rather than one end moving more in advance.

Settle for three or four steps to start with, at which point give your horse a pat, return to the circle and begin again. As the horse becomes more proficient you can gradually begin to build up the number of steps until you can comfortably achieve a dozen steps on both reins in walk. At this point you can begin to introduce the movement in trot. As the exercise becomes easier, you can ask the horse to move away from, as well as towards, the confines of your working area, or to move at an angle to the outside track with the head towards the inside or outside of the area, or on a circle. Do be careful not to allow your horse simply to go sideways without making any forwards movement as you do not want to interfere with its desire to go forwards, nor do you want the horse to start running sideways from your inside leg; if you find this happening, use a little less inside leg and support a little with the outside one, and make sure that the rein contact is not being over restrictive.

5 Pole Work

Pole work is an often neglected part of a horse's jumping work. Riders with more experienced horses too often take the attitude that it is really of benefit only to novices, and as such constitutes taking a step backwards and is therefore not worth bothering with. Those with younger animals are often tempted to rush through this stage of a horse's education in order to get it out of the way as quickly as possible and get down to the actual job of jumping over fences.

Perhaps a large part of the reason for this is that many riders are not aware that there is more than one way of tackling such work: it need not consist solely of trotting down lines of poles set at uniformly spaced distances (which ultimately proves to be as boring for the rider as it is for the horse, destroys any enthusiasm, and undermines all the good intentions that the rider may have started out with). In fact poles do not have to be in a line, or even straight, or exactly the same distance apart. There are plenty of different exercises that can be introduced to help keep the horse concentrating and prevent it from becoming complacent, whilst at the same time encouraging the rider to keep the horse moving with balance, rhythm and impulsion.

For young horses, poles obviously form a useful introduction to some kind of obstacle and help to get them used to the idea of brightly coloured objects. But this is not the sole aim of this sort of work: no matter what level the horse is at, nor whether it is sluggish or excitable in temperament, the use of poles can be of nothing but benefit if correctly carried out. It can often do a lot to help sort out many existing jumping problems as well as laying the foundations for future work with a youngster. It is worth spending some time on pole work, and recapping on it occasionally, not least because it teaches your horse to think quickly and be nimble on its feet.

The Benefits of Pole Work

- Develops co-ordination.
- Improves impulsion.
- Develops accuracy.
- Teaches the horse to adjust its length of stride without loss of balance or rhythm.
- Increases concentration and focuses the horse's attention.
- Develops discipline and obedience.
- Encourages more excitable horses to be sensible and workmanlike.

POLES

Before beginning any jumping work, you will need to spend some time warming up and loosening off your horse and, in addition to flatwork, poles on the ground can be a useful preliminary for more experienced horses and an excellent way of getting them in the right frame of mind.

It does not really matter what length your poles are for this sort of work, but if you intend to use them for jumping as well, they should ideally be around 3–3.5m (10–12ft) long. For ground poles, the heavier they are the better as they will not move around so much if the horse kicks one; for jumping work, however, it is best if they are light (while a horse that knocks a pole may be more careful the next time, it is a myth that heavy poles will make it try harder). If the horse does give itself a good knock on a heavy pole, it is far more likely to frighten it than to make it jump bigger and better.

Rustic poles will do fine if that is all you have, but since your horse is going to have to tackle coloured obstacles sooner or later, it does not take a lot of effort to get out the tins of paint and spend an hour or so jazzing them up a bit so the horse can get used to them right from the start. This of course has the added benefit of making the poles stand out better on the ground, rather than blending into it. You do not need a large number of poles; you can manage with just four, although six is better, but later on, when you begin to build grids of fences, you will need to obtain a few more.

STARTING POLE WORK

It is a good idea not to be too ambitious initially, but to start pole work by casually incorporating it into the flatwork. This is most easily done by scattering a few poles at random on the ground in your schooling area, and just walking over one occasionally. If the horse is a youngster it is a good idea to place jump wings at either end of the poles to help keep it straight and to help it get used to them.

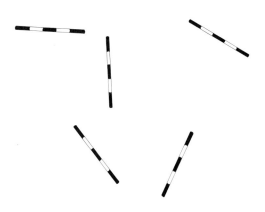

Scattered poles.

Do not feel you have to keep continually turning across to another pole, as this can make your horse feel pressured and encourage you to hurry it in order to get to the next one; take your time and just walk over a pole as and when you feel inclined to do so. This is an excellent way of helping to defuse an excitable horse and getting it into a more relaxed frame of mind: riding turns, circles, changes of rein, and even just walking near and past poles, will all give the

71

Polework will often give you a clue as to how careful a horse is likely to be over fences. Here the poles are being treated with great respect.

horse something else to think about. Walking over a pole when the horse is calm and obedient, but not necessarily expecting to do so, will also help to eliminate much of the anticipation that often causes a gassy animal to become even more so. In this particular case, bringing the horse round again and again to a pole is rarely constructive. At this stage of a novice's training, you will often find out whether the horse has any inclination to be a good jumper by the way it goes over the poles – whether it picks its feet up and is very careful, or whether it falls over them. You will also be able to pick up some clues as to what

to expect when you jump such a horse – whether it is onwards bound, stuffy, crooked, hollow, and so on.

With more excitable horses you do need to be very patient. Working them over poles day in and day out is not such a bad idea because it does teach them to regard it as work rather than a novelty and an excuse for playing the rider up, encouraging them to be a little more sensible when being ridden to fences. With this type of horse, it does not hurt to introduce poles in other situations – leave one in the paddock, for example, where you can ask the horse to walk across it each time it is turned out or

Having been through the poles a couple of times, the horse has now begun to relax a little and as a result is going forward a little better and with increased confidence.

brought in from the field. They become a part of life and cease to be associated so strongly with exciting activities. But a word of warning: do make sure the horse is led over the centre when doing this, and take care not to get in front of the horse in case it does try to put in a little jump on the first couple of occasions that it crosses it.

A lot of the time, it is not entirely the horse's fault if it does become excitable. While there are many horses that are temperamentally inclined to be like this, it is a problem often exacerbated by the rider. If you are over-anxious or start to anticipate the horse being difficult, it is easy to end up shortening the reins and hanging on to the front end, clamping your legs on and generally tensing up without even realizing you are doing it. A sensitive horse will quickly pick this up and become worried and edgy. Horses will always react to tension in the rider, and the instinctive flight mechanism takes over, which is why they will go faster when frightened. Obviously try to avoid encouraging the horse to rush in the first place, but if it does happen, do not reprimand the horse too sharply as this only upsets it further; it will begin to rush out of fear rather than excitement, and a loss of confidence is the last thing you want to happen. Rather than a sharp aid, quietly but firmly use half-halts to rebalance the horse, re-establish the walk, get the horse relaxed and responding properly to your hands and legs again before re-presenting the horse to another pole.

If your horse is going reasonably well on the flat, it should be able to maintain a certain shape over the poles, but do not become obsessed with this as it can lead to an over-dominant hand and a loss of elasticity in the gaits. It can also cause the mouth to become resistant and the horse to be so distracted by the rider that it stops concentrating on where it is putting its feet.

Try to avoid throwing the reins at the horse, whether crossing one or a line of poles. If the horse does want to stretch its neck and head forwards and down to have a good look, all well and good, and your rein contact should be elastic and fluent enough to retain the same tension while following this movement, so that the horse is not restricted. Suddenly abandoning the contact at the last moment will not make the horse stretch, and will actually upset its balance and encourage it to rush and fall on to its forehand, and probably to stumble and fall over the poles.

BUILDING UP A GRID OF POLES

There is no reason why you should not walk, trot, or even canter, over poles from time to time with a fairly slack rein, as this can, with some horses, encourage a relaxed attitude and teach it not to rely on the rider's hands for support. But this sort of contact should be established before actually approaching a pole if the horse is to remain balanced: having a contact one minute and none the next will confuse and distract the horse at the moment when it should be concentrating on the pole. This exercise does also have benefits for the rider, too, since it develops confidence and discourages the rider from making the mistake of attempting to 'pick' the horse up with the rein contact when jumping proper fences later on.

Once this stage of work is well established, and the horse is working quietly and confidently you can move on to introducing trot and canter work over the poles. It is important to ensure that you keep the rhythm and tempo regular and, especially when you start cantering, try to avoid 'seeing a stride' for a pole, but rather concentrate on maintaining a balanced and level stride and allowing the horse to gauge it for itself. As before, do incorporate this work into other flatwork exercises and do not feel that you have to stay in the same gait all the time. This is particularly important when riding more excitable horses, as spells spent in walk will have a tremendously relaxing and calming effect.

If the horse is a little spooky to start with, there is nothing to worry about, provided you keep the horse moving with impulsion and rhythm into the bridle so that it gains confidence from your attitude and does not learn to duck out to one side of the pole. If anything, this is a good quality in a showjumper as it usually means that it will be very careful. But you need to be tactful as well as firm, since hurrying the horse could lead to its becoming frightened. Unlike professional show jumpers, amateurs have a big advantage in that there is not the same

A useful exercise with a more experienced horse is to canter through a line of poles (or even over single poles) with a slack rein. The mare here is coping well, finding her own balance rather than relying on her rider for support.

sort of pressure to produce results quickly, so there is no real excuse for not taking as much time as the horse needs to grow in confidence in itself and trust in its rider.

When you are satisfied with its progress over single poles, you can begin to introduce more complex exercises. The next step is to arrange three or four poles in a line parallel to each other at a distance of approximately 2.5m (9ft) apart. Spacing them like this to start with will mean that, should the horse become a little uptight or excited and attempt to jump or canter through them, it will not get into difficulties (as might happen if they are placed closer together). Continue the horse's education by walking and trotting through these and, if its schooling is advanced enough, canter over them too. If the horse tends to get excited, be careful not to do too much canter work over the poles; spend time in walk again, getting it settled.

Once again, ride circles, turns and changes of rein, rather than continually going over the poles, and do work over them from both directions. As the horse's work becomes more consistent, you can increase the number of poles to six, which will require a more sustained physical and mental effort. While working in trot, you will probably find it best to continue rising as it is easier to stay in balance and to help regulate the rhythm and tempo if the horse tries to speed up. It will also allow the horse to use its back freely and comfortably so it is less inclined to hollow. The exception to this is with a rather stuffy horse, when working over poles while sitting to the trot – provided you are supple enough – will help you to motivate him more, especially if the horse tends to anticipate cantering when you adopt this position.

Should you find that, although you meet the poles with the horse working well, the horse meets the first one awkwardly – either fitting in an extra, short and shuffling stride, or alternatively a longer, unbalanced one at the last moment, which breaks the rhythm of the gait – try turning towards them from a different distance away. This should help you to meet them on a better stride, rather than allow the horse to become behind or in front of the hand and leg. It will also help you to begin to see a good stride so that you can plan your approaches better and find a good take-off point when it comes to jumping later on.

VARIETY

Because boredom must be avoided, pole work exercises must be kept varied and imaginative, otherwise the horse will end up switching off completely, or else anticipating the next move, neither of which is desirable. There are many different ways of working around and over the poles while they are set out at 2.5m (9ft) distances, some of which you will find more demanding than others, but do try to avoid becoming repetitive; ring the changes on them frequently. You do not need to ride continually across the centres of them. A good exercise, especially with a horse that tends to rush or anticipate, is to progress only a certain distance along and then to ride a half-circle, either to the left or right, rather than continuing to the end. You can also try riding upward and downward transitions through them. Make sure that your aids are never abrupt, but do give yourself some kind of target, such as walking over pole 1, trotting over poles 2, 3 and 4 and then walking again over poles 5 and 6 so that you begin to establish the habit of discipline, obedience and accuracy at all times and in all circumstances.

Length of Stride

Do not fall into the trap of equating size of horse with length of stride. A big 16.2hh horse can actually have the same length of stride as one that is 15.2hh if it has short legs in relation to its frame, or a very upright shoulder. Although you do eventually want to teach the horse to lengthen or shorten its stride, this is something you need to work on as the horse is ready for it; attempting to ask for too much before it is able to cope can lead to loss of confidence, balance and elasticity in his steps.

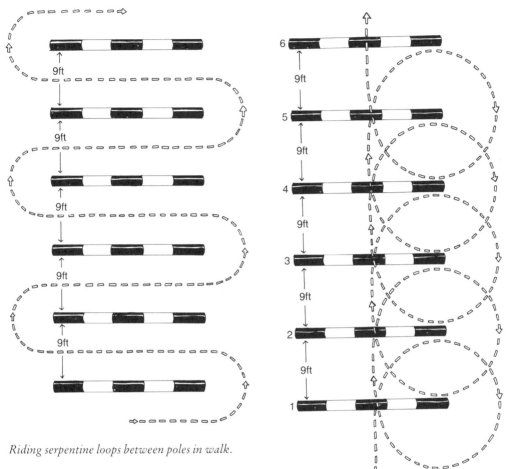

Riding serpentine loops between poles in walk.

Circling over poles in walk.

Riding serpentine loops at walk in and out of the poles is another good way of settling an excitable horse as well as encouraging more suppleness and preparing your horse for more demanding exercises. When you feel that the horse can manage these loops in a reasonably good balance, begin to introduce some circles. Combined with the poles, circles will help to increase activity in the quarters and improve general suppleness; they will also promote a better balanced, rounder and more athletic stride. With horses that rush or tend to be lazy, the improvement in impulsion, balance and concentration can be considerable once you have completed the exercise once or twice.

Start off by walking straight over pole 1, then ride a small circle to the right without crossing pole 2; return to the centre of pole 1, walk over it and continue to pole 2, walking over it and circling away to the right again without

77

Rosie is often a little complacent about poles on the ground, but the circling exercise works wonders with her. Since it is a fairly demanding exercise, she has to concentrate and pay more attention to what she is doing. It also encourages Nina to ride more accurately and positively.

crossing either poles 1 or 3. Continue like this along the line of poles. Although it seems a pretty straightforward exercise at first glance, you will find that it is actually a lot more demanding than it appears and to start with you may find it hard to maintain rhythm and balance. However, improvement comes quickly.

Do make sure that you cross the centres of the poles each time, rather than the ends. Ask the horse to bend correctly around your inside leg. If necessary use a slightly open rein aid to do this, but do not exaggerate this, or draw the hand backwards, as this will restrict forward impulsion and also encourage the horse

to try to pivot around the inside foreleg with its weight on the forehand instead of engaging its quarters correctly.

Watch that the quarters or shoulders do not drift out of the circle. Guard against this by thinking about pushing the horse forward and around each circle rather than pulling it round and keeping a positive contact on the outside rein. The outside leg should be ready to prevent or correct any crookedness. If your horse finds it hard to cope initially, you can make it a little easier for it until it is more supple by circling over alternate poles rather than each one. Repeat the exercise on both reins so the horse does

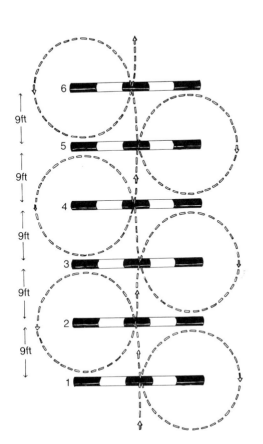

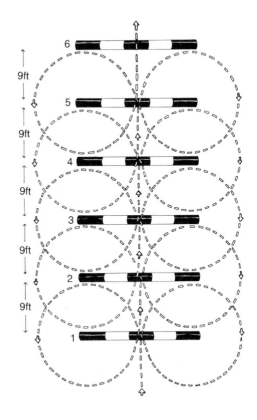

Riding a figure of eight over each pole in walk.

Circling in alternate directions over alternate poles in walk.

not become one-sided, and then try varying the exercise by circling to the left over one pole, to the right over the next, and so on. The changes of rein will keep the horse thinking and attending to the rider, as well as better at accepting changes of bend.

You can make this exercise more demanding still by riding a figure of eight movement over each pole before moving on to the next one. This requires even more precision of movement. Make sure you meet each pole straight at the centre,

rather than diagonally. These exercises should only be ridden at the walk, as it will be too tight for the horse to attempt them in other gaits, but it is possible to adapt them to accommodate trot work.

Instead of circling over single poles, circle over pairs of poles instead: trot over poles 1 and 2, circle back round over poles 1 and 2, and progress on to poles 3 and 4, circle round over poles 3 and 4 but without crossing 1, 2, 5 or 6 and so on. Having ridden three circles to the right in this fashion, try the exercise circling to the left, then alternate left and right circles and finally try figure of eight movements over them. You will find

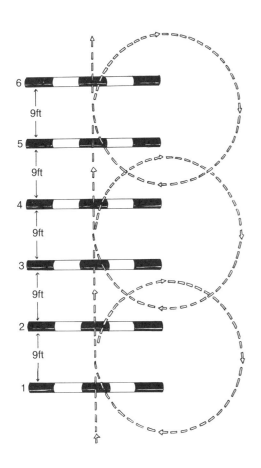

6

9ft

5

9ft

4

9ft

3

9ft

2

9ft

1

Circling over pairs of poles in trot.

going. If the horse has to put in awkward shuffling half-steps or throw its front legs forward and lunge over them, the distance is not quite correct and will need altering.

INCREASING ACTIVITY

As your horse trots over the more closely placed poles, you will notice an increased bounciness in its step; this is caused by a more elevated stride and greater activity in the back. Be prepared for this and try to stay with the movement, because getting left behind and bumping down into the saddle will cause the horse to hollow, especially if you catch the mouth at the same time. Over-anticipation and tipping forwards in front of the movement is just as bad because it will make your legs ineffective and push the horse on to its forehand, so try to strike a happy medium. Once you have been over them once or twice you will know better just what to expect and should be able to find a good balance.

If you have a horse that is inclined to be lazy, brush up on the flatwork, insisting that the horse does go forward from the leg (*see* Chapter 4) and, if necessary, give the horse a little tap with your whip just behind your leg each time it goes over a pole. A long dressage whip is ideal for this purpose, since you do not have to take one hand off the reins in order to use it, thus making it easier to keep the horse straight.

Asking for some lengthened strides when your horse is ready is a useful exercise, particularly with a stuffy horse. This can be done by trotting diagonally across the poles at their shorter distances,

yourself with plenty to think about, even though you are working over pairs of poles rather than single ones as the increase of pace will make it just as demanding to negotiate successfully.

As you both become more proficient, you can begin to work in trot over poles that are more closely placed together at a distance of approximately 1.2–1.5m (4–5ft) apart. Be prepared to adjust the distance between the poles according to the size of the horse and its length of stride, as well as the way the horse is which saves having to fiddle around re-arranging them. The great advantage of using poles for this sort of work is that you can keep the horse balanced right from the start, and discourage any tendency to run instead of lengthening properly. When the horse is lengthening properly, the steps behind will be of the same length as those in front.

Another useful exercise that helps to keep the horse thinking and responding quickly to the aids, is to place the poles at angles to each other so that the length of stride can be varied while trotting across them. When going across the centre, the distance between them is the same, but if

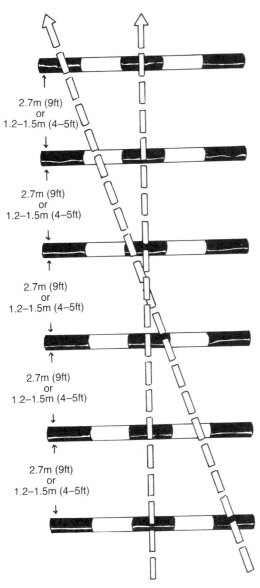

2.7m (9ft)
or
1.2–1.5m (4–5ft)

2.7m (9ft)
or
1.2–1.5m (4–5ft)

2.7m (9ft)
or
1.2–1.5m (4–5ft)

2.7m (9ft)
or
1.2–1.5m (4–5ft)

2.7m (9ft)
or
1.2–1.5m (4–5ft)

Poles may be set at distances of approximately 2.7m (9ft) apart and ridden across the centres in walk, trot or canter. Alternatively set them at about 1.2–1.5m (4–5ft) apart and ride across the centre, or take a diagonal line (to lengthen the stride) in trot.

Poles set at angles to each other.

Plastic cones with square ends have been used to raise the ends of the poles producing more activity and athleticism in the trot. It is also encouraging Inky to think very carefully about where he is placing his feet. Nina is riding in good balance here and allowing Inky to lower and stretch his head and neck freely.

you trot along the edges instead you can alternately ask the horse to lengthen and shorten the stride; this is very good for sharpening up your own reactions as well.

Helping to increase flexion of the joints can also be achieved when moving straight through the line of poles by the simple expedient of raising alternate ends of each of the poles on to bricks or Bloks. This will develop a better hock and shoulder action, which encourages the horse to use the ground as a springboard from which it pushes itself in an upward and forward direction.

Obviously, this is not an exhaustive list of pole work exercises, but it should at least give you a few ideas as to just what can be done with them, and how they can be made more or less demanding, according to the level the horse is working at and what you are trying to achieve. You will find that you can even combine some of the exercises – for example, trotting a circle over the first pair of poles, and then cantering over the remaining poles in a straight line. There is no reason why pole work should ever be boring for either you or your horse – a little imagination can go a long way.

6 Fences and Distances

At shows you will come across a variety of different fences, such as walls, gates, coloured fillers, planks and stiles. Obviously it is an advantage to be able to practise over such obstacles at home in order to give the horse some experience of them before meeting them in competition. They can be expensive to buy, although if you are good at DIY you may be able to put together a small set more cheaply. If you have neither the time, the money nor the expertise, one solution is to hire the facilities at a local equestrian centre, where you will have both the time and the equipment available to round out your horse's education and sort out any problems with particular fences. Hiring such facilities is often made cheaper and easier if you can get together with a few friends, since you can not only split the cost between you, but take it in turns to alter and put up fences for each other.

For schooling at home, and in particular

It need not cost a fortune to hire facilities at a local equestrian centre if you split the cost between yourself and a few friends. Jumping on unfamiliar ground over unfamiliar fences is good experience for a youngster.

for gymnastic work, you do not need a huge range of different fences, however. You will need plenty of poles, obviously, but variety can be introduced by altering the shape of the fences, their distance from each other and the use of poles on the ground to encourage a more athletic effort and better technique. If you are fortunate enough to own, or have the use of, fillers and planks, and so on, there is no reason why you should not incorporate them as elements of a grid, although you should make sure that the highest part of each can be dislodged if you hit it. With youngsters it is probably best to stick to simpler fences constructed of poles initially until more confidence and experience is gained.

Someone experienced on the ground can be helpful if you have a problem. This is especially advisable if you are riding a green horse or if young children are jumping, in case of an accident, but nine times out of ten you can usually manage quite satisfactorily on your own – provided you observe sensible safety precautions. Sometimes working alone can be an advantage, because if the horse does knock a pole down, or you want to change something around, the time spent having to get off and lead the horse across to the fence, set it right, remount, and trot a few circles to get the horse going again actually has a beneficial effect as it gives the horse a chance to relax. An assistant on the ground may mean that you do not have to do so much legwork, but it can result in your keeping

An assistant on hand to help adjust fences for you is helpful but not essential. Sometimes, having to cope on your own does give the horse a much-needed breathing space.

a lot of psychological pressure on your horse to keep coming down to a fence or series of fences and to perform well over them, which can make a horse very uptight. So often, it is a good idea to allow the horse to recover mentally and unwind every now and then – especially if the horse is an excitable type – rather than to keep asking questions of him. When you have a quick and efficient helper on hand it is frequently tempting to keep pressing on instead, even against your better judgement.

EQUIPMENT

From the convenience point of view, it is much easier to deal with fences that are easy to move around and alter – particularly if you are coping on your own. But while you do not want them to be so heavy or awkward to shift that they give you a hernia, neither should they be so light and flimsy that the slightest puff of wind blows them down, or the first touch of a hoof reduces them to matchwood.

As far as poles are concerned, although you can make do with surprisingly little, it is better to have too many than too few. They should be around 3–3.5m (10–12ft) in length so as to give a more inviting appearance, and preferably they should all be uniform in length as this will cause fewer problems when building fences or grids. It is also best if they are rounded with a smooth surface because square sections or projections can cause injuries. They should look fairly solid in appearance, with a minimum diameter of 9cm (3½in) for good visibility and to encourage respect. However, you should avoid using very heavy poles, not just because they are hard work to lift, but because if the horse does hit one you want him to approach it and try to jump it again, not hurt itself so badly that it is frightened off. For this reason, poles should not be wedged in between wings either. Horses are either careful or careless, and although touching a pole may encourage a horse to make a better effort on its next attempt, no amount of bashing will change its basic attitude.

There is a theory that horses are colour blind. Yet it is a strange thing that some of the best and boldest hunters in the world will not trot over a single, small, coloured filler because they are frightened of it, although they will quite happily tackle a similar rustic obstacle. So this theory may well be a misconception. Whether they are colour blind or not, horses do react differently to coloured as opposed to rustic fences. Since your horse will have to deal with coloured fences at competitions, it is important to get it used to them. It is cheaper to buy plain poles, but it does not take a great deal of time or effort to brighten them up yourself with the paintbrush. They will also be more easily visible, but do remember that whether indoors or out, artificial light or bright sunshine reflected from newly painted fences may make your horse spook, especially if the paint is white.

Good wings to support poles exactly where you want them are ideal and help to draw the horse towards the centre of each fence, but upright stands are quite acceptable and easier to move around, as well as cheaper to buy. It is essential to use correct cups: planks and gates should be hung on flat cups, while rounded poles should rest on round cups. If you put a plank or gate on a rounded cup it will not fall if the horse touches it and

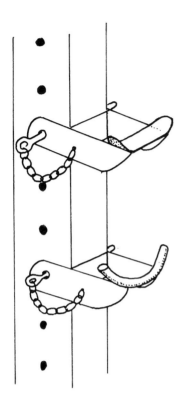

Flat jump cups (top) and rounded jump cups (bottom).

may bring down either the wings, the horse, or both. Rounded cups should be reasonably shallow, not so deep that it is difficult for the poles to be dislodged from them. Never jump a fence, or ride between wings that have jump cups on but no pole resting on them as this can lead to nasty injuries. When they are not in use, put them well out of harm's way where the horse cannot stand on them and the rider cannot fall off on them.

Cavaletti – long poles bolted to a large cross at each end – were commonly used until recent years, but should never be employed as they are far too dangerous; if the horse hits one the apparatus will tend to roll and can become entangled with the horse's legs, and if the rider should fall off and land on one of the crosses at the end, the injuries caused can be serious. A more modern innovation, which has replaced cavaletti, are Bloks. These are made of a moulded plastic and are very durable, tough and light to handle; they are still not entirely ideal, but they are certainly a big improvement.

SITE

Where you site your fences is as important as the type and combinations you build. With a more experienced horse – especially if you plan to do some cross-country work with it – it can be a good idea to teach him to jump safely and competently on both upwards and downwards gradients, but you should remember that this will affect the length of stride. On a downhill gradient the horse will land with a longer stride than normal, while a jump on an upward slope will cause the horse to adopt a shorter stride than usual, and you will need to take this into account any succeeding fences.

For most purposes, however, it is best to select an area that is as level as possible, since this will be more conducive to teaching the horse to move with balance and rhythm. Going downhill, the horse will tend to drop on to its forehand, making the horse likely to hit fences with its forelegs; uphill, the horse may get very strung out and fail to bring its quarters sufficiently beneath it, which will cause it to jump very flat.

Even though the ground may be level, it will not always make for ideal jumping conditions. If the take-off and landing

Country Jumpkins, a relatively new product, but very useful for schooling purposes and allowing fences to be built up to a height of 5ft 11in (1.8m) if wished. They are extremely versatile and light to move around, very durable, safe, and can be stacked on top of each other for easy storage. (Photo: courtesy of Baker-Mac.)

areas become very poached, as will happen in wet weather, it will affect the horse's length of stride, tending to shorten it; the clinging qualities will also serve to slow and sap the horse's impulsion, making it difficult for it to push off the ground and can result in strains and over-reaches. When the ground gets into this state it is best avoided. Moving your fences around regularly will help to prevent really deep, boggy areas from developing. Hard ground can also pose a problem and will cause a lot of jarring on the horse's forelegs. Putting sand, shavings or peat down on the approaches and landings will help to soften some of the impact, although it should extend far enough on each side of the fence so that it does not create the effect of a false groundline. In such conditions, it is also sensible to keep your jumping schooling to a minimum and over smaller fences, since even if your horse does not go lame as a result of the continual jarring, its legs can soon become sore and this will cause it to jump poorly, if not actually to refuse altogether.

One other thing that can affect the horse's attitude and length of stride is the direction in which you are jumping, that is towards or away from the exit/ entrance to your schooling area. Generally, most horses are more onwards bound when heading towards the exit and less so when moving away from it. This is also a point worth bearing in mind at shows, not just at home.

GROUNDLINES

Horses assess the height of a fence from the base upwards, so clearly defined groundlines are a good idea as they help the horse to judge its take-off point more accurately. A groundline may be formed by a drop-pole beneath the top rail, by a single pole on the ground, or even by a coloured filler or line of straw bales (the latter two can also often encourage the horse to lower its head, take a better look at the fence when approaching and judge the size better). Unless you are using a placing pole, never leave an open gap between the top of a fence and the ground as it makes it very difficult for the horse to judge its jump, it is less than inviting, which can soon lead to a loss of confidence. Never attempt to deceive the horse by setting a 'false' groundline with the lower elements drawn back behind a vertical line dropped from the front of the fence. This will simply encourage the horse to believe that the top of the fence is above the groundline, judge its take-off point accordingly, and get too close to the fence. While ideally, you want the horse to come in fairly deep as opposed to standing off, you do not want it to get so far underneath the fence that it cannot extricate itself and continually hits the fence with its forearms or knees.

Large oil drums are commonly used as a means of filling in the space beneath a fence, but this can actually be very dangerous since they will roll if they are knocked and could bring the horse down, although used standing on their ends and weighted with water or sand they can form useful wings. If they are used with a pole resting on the top, the pole should be positioned towards the rim so that it can be easily dislodged. Old tyres are another hazard and should not be used propped against a pole as a horse can put a foot through and become trapped.

UPRIGHTS AND SPREADS

The shape of a fence will dictate the shape that a horse makes over it. Basically they can all be divided into two categories: 'vertical' or 'upright' fences, and 'spreads'. With an upright fence, the take-off point will be the same distance from the fence as the landing point on the other side, and the highest point of the horse's flight will be directly over the top of it. Over a spread fence, the distance between fence and landing point will be greater than it is between take-off point and the fence, and the arc described by the horse will be longer and shallower, with the highest point of flight being either close to, or over, the back rail (depending on the type of spread). These factors will influence the horse's length of stride when landing as well as its shape in the air: the steeper the landing, the more on its forehand the horse will be and the shorter the next stride; the further the landing is away from the fence, the longer the next stride. Although it will not make much discernible difference over small fences, it will become much more apparent over large fences, so you

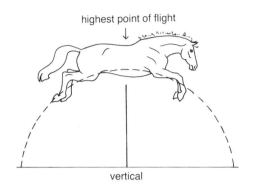

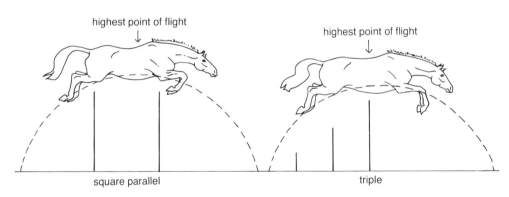

The shape of a fence will affect the shape a horse makes over it, and also dictate ideal take-off and landing points. Over a vertical (top) the arc made by the horse will be much deeper and, provided the approach is correct, the take-off and landing points will be approximately the same distance from the fence. With a square parallel the horse takes off closer to the front of the fence – with the highest point of flight being either over, or close to, the back rail – and lands further out from the fence than from a vertical. The increased distance the horse has to cover from take-off to landing means that the arc is shallower, but it is required to really go forward in the air and to use its back end well. With a triple (bottom right), the horse has to get even closer to the front of the fence, the highest point of flight will be over the back rail, and it will land further away from the fence than it would from a parallel (having described an even shallower arc). Unless the horse has been ridden in deeply and correctly, a triple can encourage a certain amount of flattening. When jumping spreads, the horse will also require a little more pace than for a vertical, and it will also have the effect of carrying him on more after landing.

will need to make allowances for it when measuring out distances between combinations of different fences. This is important if the horse is to meet each one on a good stride and not get too close or be encouraged to stand off. Varying the

type of fence in a grid can also help to increase or decrease the horse's impulsion and stride at a given point, according to what you want to achieve.

Probably the simplest of upright fences is a cross-pole. This is very useful

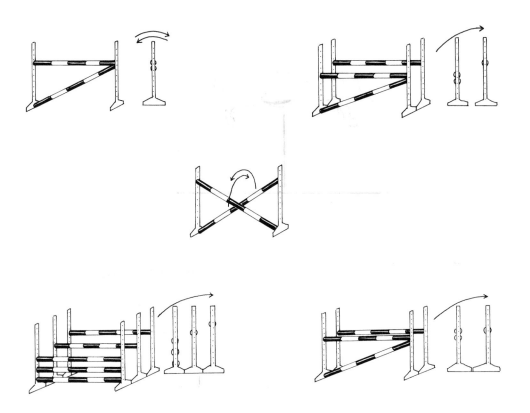

Different fences, which you can use in a grid, and the directions from which they can be jumped. Vertical, ascending spread, parallel, triple (clockwise from top left) and crosspole (centre).

for a young horse or one that tends to jump crookedly, as it encourages the horse to tackle the lowest part at the centre, while the higher edges encourage it to tuck its feet up a little more carefully. Cross-poles need not always be uprights; they can be built in the form of spread fences, too. Since spreads encourage a longer and more shallow arc, they can help to get the horse going forward a little more in the air rather than awkwardly jumping straight up and straight down. Especially in the case of parallels, when made wider rather than higher, they really get the horse to jump

correctly, using its head, neck and back. They also encourage the rider to give the horse freedom to stretch its head and neck, which is absolutely vital.

True parallels – where the top rails at the front and back are the same height – are probably one of the most beneficial fences in helping to develop a good technique, but they can present problems for a young horse who may think at first that the fence is an upright until it suddenly sees the back rail at the last moment. Until a young horse has gained more experience and confidence, it may be best to start off with the front rail a little

This picture shows very well just how deep you need to get to the front of a triple bar in order to jump it successfully. You can also see just how hard the hocks are working and how much strain is put on them when the horse is going correctly – hence the importance of good conformation.

The same horse in the air and beginning to land over the same fence. It is using its back end extremely well, and it is being allowed to travel freely forwards by the rider's keeping her seat a little out of the saddle.

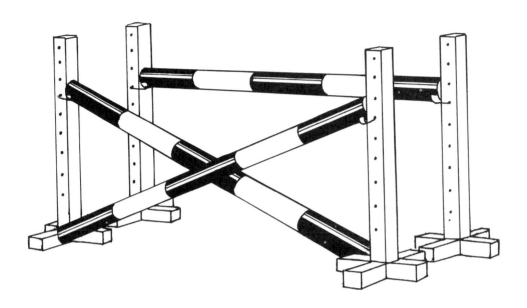

The back rail is easily visible, making this a good fence for introducing a youngster to the concept of jumping width as well as height. However, once the horse has gained in experience, it should not be used too frequently as it is very easy for a horse to get lazy over it. It also encourages the horse to be slack with the front legs and to get its height too late. A square parallel is the most beneficial spread fence for gymnastic work as it makes the horse snap up its front legs more tightly.

lower than the back one so that it can see clearly what is required. When building spreads of any type, the back rail should never be lower than the front one, and it is best to use only one pole as the last element of a parallel so as to minimize the risk of injury should the horse fail to make the distance across it. Planks should never be used as a substitute for the back rail of a spread fence.

APPROACH

It is important to try to approach each fence squarely and at the centre of it. Jumping a spread fence at an angle can make it considerably wider and, if tackling a combination of fences, the distance will be altered between each, making it more tricky for the horse and presenting it with a poor take-off point. There is also an increased risk of the horse running out at the fence or, if it does jump it, knocking the rider's legs against the wings.

You should also try to arrive at each fence in a steady, balanced way so that the horse has every opportunity to clear it, ideally getting fairly close to the base so that the horse sits back on its hocks and really uses its back end to push itself up into the air. If the horse is allowed to run on into the fence, with its hocks trailing instead of engaged beneath, it will tend to throw itself over with the result that it may not be able to make the height or width. The horse will almost certainly land with even less balance than it had on the approach, and it will be ill-prepared for a second obstacle. Being able to achieve a good approach is to a large extent down to good, thorough preparation on the flat and over poles.

DISTANCES

Distances need to be carefully measured out so that your horse meets each fence at the optimum take-off point; stride it out on your own feet by all means but take the precaution of using a tape measure as well to check on your distances until you can get them right consistently.

As a general rule of thumb, it is safe to work on the principle that the length of stride of an average horse in canter is around 3.5m (12ft), and that it will take off approximately 1.2–1.8m (4–6ft) away from the fence itself. As discussed, the take-off point will be slightly further away from a vertical than it will be from a spread, and the lower the front element of a spread, the closer the ideal take-off point will be. Using this knowledge, you can work out approximately the correct distance between placing poles and fences, and between combinations of fences. Thus, for one non-jumping canter stride between two similar fences, for example two verticals or two parallels,

Get used to striding out distances between fences and poles (this will also help you to gauge related distances at shows), but do try to make the length of your steps consistent so that you can set up the correct distances for your horse each time.

This shows the importance of getting the distances for your placing poles right. This one is so far away that this horse, Friday, has had to stand off – not exactly an ideal situation in view of the fact that she is tackling a spread and now has a tremendous distance to cover to the landing side.

The next time through the same combination, Friday was not prepared to be so bold and propped on to her forehand on the approach, putting in an extra stride between the placing pole and the fence. Although it had the effect of bringing her in to a closer and more manageable take-off point, she had broken her rhythm, lost all her forward impulsion (note how the hocks are trailing) and consequently put in a very sticky, awkward jump, which probably worried her just as much as the previous attempt.

the ideal distance would be around 7.3m (24ft); for two non-jumping strides add on 3.5m (12ft) giving a total of 11m (36ft) between elements, and so on, measuring the distances between fences from the back rail of the first part to the front rail of the next jump.

This is not, however, a hard and fast rule. These distances are necessarily approximate, although it does give you a basis from which to start. A small pony with a shorter canter stride might be happier with a shorter distance between fences, and a big, long-striding horse, would probably benefit from a longer distance, so do be prepared to observe the results you are getting and to adjust these distances slightly to suit the individual. Be careful not to ask your horse to cope with very long strides before it is ready, and even then not too often, as having to really stretch to reach each fence will teach the horse to jump flat, and for showjumping you want the horse to round over its fences; if anything a slightly shorter distance will encourage a better knee and shoulder action. In both cases, whether asking your horse to extend or shorten itself in order to reach the optimum take-off point, take into acount that all horses are individuals, and do not ask too much of it too soon. Some

It is possible to see here the effect that trotting into a fence has on the length of stride on landing. The distance between these two fences is 24ft (7.3m), which Friday normally succeeds in covering reasonably comfortably in one non-jumping stride when approaching the first fence in canter. When approaching the first fence in trot, however, despite the fact that Pat is driving her forwards with great determination, the distance is too long and her stride is only just taking her beyond the pole placed at half-way between the two fences. She will be forced either to put in an extra little stride or to stand off in order to clear the second fence. A more suitable distance for this horse doing this exercise would have been around 20–21ft (6–6.4m). You should also remember that when jumping smaller fences, you will not be carried so far in to the next obstacle.

Jumping from a vertical to a spread: the horse lands more closely to the base of the vertical so that it has to take a longer stride between the two elements before taking off for the parallel. In fact, in this sequence it ends up having to stand off the spread. For this horse, with this combination of dissimilar fences, a shorter distance between the two fences would have encouraged a more athletic effort over the spread from a closer take-off point.

Compare these pictures of jumping from a spread to a vertical with the previous sequence on pages 96–7, which shows them in the opposite order. The distance between the fences is exactly the same, but the increased momentum from jumping the spread, together with the horse's landing further out from the base, carries the horse on and brings it in deeper to the second fence and to a more ideal take-off point. This requires it to rebalance itself quickly and make a good effort to pick its front end up.

may find it easier to fly over longer distances, although it can lead to inaccuracy and poor technique. But even though a shorter distance will teach a horse to shorten and jump more correctly, if it has already got into the habit of jumping long and flat you are not going to change its style overnight, and tightening up distances too rapidly will discourage or frighten it, so aim for improvement over a period of time.

There are two other points you will need to bear in mind when setting up a grid of fences. Firstly, the gait at which you are approaching it: if jumping from a trot, the first canter stride on landing will be much shorter than if you had approached the fence in canter, and the distance between the first and second fence will therefore need to be shortened by approximately 90cm (3ft). Secondly, especially as you begin to tackle larger fences, you will begin to find that the type of fences will influence the distances set between combinations of dissimilar obstacles. For example, as discussed earlier in this chapter, the horse will land further out from a spread than from a vertical, so that it may be necessary to increase the distance between the two, and when jumping from a vertical to a spread, to shorten the distance slightly. You will discover a certain amount of this with experience and from observing other horses jumping, but if in doubt use a pole on the ground first before erecting a fence in its place to check that your judgement is not too far out.

If you use bounce fences, there is no canter stride between each element; the horse lands and takes off again straight away. It can be a useful combination for getting the horse to think and react a little more quickly and to make it more supple in its back, but care does need to be taken with the distances between the elements. If you are approaching from trot, allow a distance of 2.7–3.4m (9–11ft); from canter allow 3.4–4.2m (11–14ft). Start off small, and never attempt bounce fences with a very inexperienced horse or one that is excitable or over-confident in case it attempts to treat it as a spread fence.

7 Introducing Grids

Grids – or lines of fences – are used as a means of allowing the horse to learn how to adjust its stride and balance, to use itself correctly over fences, and to build up its confidence.

Before starting on any jumping, do sufficient work on the flat to loosen your horse off and ensure that it is obedient and concentrating. However, bear in mind that if you overdo it (particularly with a youngster) it can make the animal dull and cause just as many problems as insufficient preparation. Doing some polework is often a useful preliminary to jumping as it helps to focus the horse's attention as well as promoting a good rhythm and activity. With a young horse that has not yet begun any jumping work, it is an advantage to introduce it to poles on the ground before progressing to single fences; and only when it is confident over these single fences should you move on to introducing successive fences in a line.

Actually getting off the ground for the first time is an unusual feeling for a youngster and it will often jump bigger and rounder initially than the size of the fence deserves. If, however, you find that the opposite is the case and that it is a little lacking in spring and rather clumsy to start with, do not despair as it may well be caused by weakness and immaturity, not necessarily by lack of ability. It should improve with time and work as it becomes stronger and learns how to engage its hocks better; but in either instance, until it has developed a degree of co-ordination, confidence and begun to find its balance on landing, it is best to stick to single fences rather than upset it by making demands that it may not be ready for or capable of meeting.

When you first introduce a fence to your horse, it is usually best done by starting off with a placing pole in front of a small cross-pole and riding into it in trot. The placing pole should be at a distance of approximately 2.7m (9ft) from the base of the jump, although this distance may vary very slightly according to the horse's size and length of stride. You may also find that an enthusiastic horse will try to take off from in front of the placing pole to begin with, in which case move the pole further away from the fence so that it does have to step over it; when it gets the idea you can gradually move it back to a more desirable distance. Using a placing pole is invaluable in helping the horse to find the correct take-off point so that it grows in confidence and does not frighten itself by having to put in a huge jump because it has taken off from too far away or has got too close and has to catjump (or even stop) to get itself out of trouble. It is therefore important to position the pole so that the horse will be comfortable. Never attempt to trap the horse by putting it impossibly close, nor make the horse flatten and rush by having to reach over a very long distance.

A cross-pole is probably the best fence to use initially as it generally has an inviting appearance and the higher sides

Do not try to get too complicated too soon. A small cross-pole is ideal as an introduction to jumping for a young horse or as a warm-up fence for a more experienced one. The placing pole in front of it means that the horse meets the fence at a good take-off point each time. Friday is going forward to this fence in a good rhythm and balance, and without rushing, while Pat is at this moment in a good position although she could be allowing her hands to travel forward more, allowing more freedom of the headcarriage.

do encourage the horse to lift its knees; it also draws the horse into the lowest and central part of the fence right from the start, which is obviously the ideal place for the horse to be. This means that the rider has to do less fiddling on the last part of the approach to ensure that the horse is straight; fiddling can distract the horse, interfere with its jump, and possibly cause it to hollow.

Before approaching the fence, establish a good, even and steady gait. The same rule applies to more experienced horses and to more demanding fences, as much as to novices, but it is surprising how discipline, common sense and patience can fly out the window when a fence suddenly appears. If you are not happy with your approach, circle away

in plenty of time and get it sorted out; then, having achieved a good rhythm in your working trot you can approach the fence with everything in your favour. Do not fuss overmuch about outline. Even if your horse can work in a good outline, on the bit, it has to be at an extremely high level of training to be able to jump a fence successfully from this shape. As can be seen from the pictures illustrating the sequence of jumping on pages 12–13 of this book, a horse needs to be able to adjust its headcarriage at each phase in order to be able to use it to the maximum. If its head and neck are being pushed into a very tight shape it will not have the freedom to do this and will be unable to balance properly, with consequent loss of confidence.

As with trotting poles, it is best to stay in a rising trot as it helps to maintain a good rhythm and the horse is less inclined to anticipate canter. Do try very hard not to see a stride into a placing pole, nor to ride positively to the pole and then freeze in front of the fence; nor should you give the horse a sudden kick just as you reach it. Concentrate instead on maintaining rhythm and impulsion, sitting quietly, keeping your leg on and allowing the pole to do the work instead of trying to do it all yourself. You have to allow the horse to think for itself and work it out, which sounds easy enough in principle, but it is surprising how few riders are prepared to do this in practice, unable to resist the temptation to fiddle and try to 'help' the horse, when in fact it quite often does nothing of the sort. Your job is to present the horse correctly to the fence, but do so as unobtrusively and quietly as possible, with an absolute minimum of interference. Allow the horse to make its own mistakes instead of making them for it, so that it learns how best to help itself, and to be quick-witted.

As mentioned earlier, some youngsters will jump rather higher than the height of the fence would seem to justify, so be ready to go with the horse and ensure that your hands move forward and down allowing it freedom to use its head and neck correctly. Do not try to anticipate this and throw your weight forward in an exaggerated manner, though, as this will serve only to unbalance the horse and cause it to quicken its step, falling on to its forehand at the same time. As a result, the horse will be unable to use its shoulders correctly, which will also lead to problems such as rushing and standing off.

THE RIDER'S POSITION

At this point, it is worth pausing briefly to spend a moment or two considering the rider's position, as this can influence the horse's style considerably, whether it is a novice or a more advanced animal. While most people probably have a fair idea of what constitutes a 'perfect' position over a fence, few stop to think about the adverse effects that a less than adequate

Personal Style

Everyone tends to develop their own style to a certain extent, and there is no point in being able to sit beautifully in a classic textbook position if it means that you are completely ineffective or totally at sea when on a strange or awkward horse. But you do need to be able to differentiate between good and bad style. Even though it may not conform perfectly to textbook ideals, it must be secure, balanced and effective; the rider must have a feel for the horse and an ability to adapt and ride accordingly. The rider's style must not hamper it, and it must be consistent – even under the pressure of competition.

This picture shows a position which is not far off being perfect. Ross is in good balance with a nice contact, allowing the horse to use itself with the minimum of interference. The front legs of the horse are in a good position, the head and neck is low, and the horse is really rounding and using itself.

position can cause. It is only bad or poor riders who do not bother to check on themselves, and while it is true that not all jumping problems in horses stem from poor rider technique, it is fair to say that more than a few can be traced back in origin to this. It is up to you as the rider to obtain and maintain the horse's confidence and develop its ability, not just in the selection of obstacles and placing poles but also in your manner of riding to, over and away from fences. None of us is perfect, but it is grossly unfair to expect a horse to keep producing of its best time and time again if its

rider is actively hampering it, whether it is intentional or not.

Some of the commonest problems that can result from the rider's adoption of a less orthodox style, and that can adversely affect the horse's athletic potential or cause setback in its training, include the following:

Head and Trunk

Collapsed Ribcage:

Often accompanied by rounded shoulders, the rider is dependent on the

Repeatedly getting left behind – especially if you hang onto the horse's mouth when it happens – can cause the horse to hollow in anticipation of the discomfort, thus undoing any of the good you may have achieved through using gymnastic work. However, it does happen on occasion – as with Ross at this water jump – but he has tried to ensure that his upper body stays with the horse as much as possible, and he has had the presence of mind to open his arms and push his hands forwards to give the horse total freedom of its head and neck. Thus, despite having got left behind, the horse is still able to use itself properly and without being restricted. The better your position is initially, the easier it is to react correctly like this if you do make a mistake in judging the horse's take-off point.

horse's stability and honesty to stay in the saddle. It can be quite a common habit, especially when beginning to tackle larger fences and will unbalance the horse, putting it on its forehand for longer when landing and allowing less free-moving horses to fade away.

Anticipating:

Anticipating a fence and starting to fold forwards too soon can confuse and upset a horse considerably, causing it to panic and take off too early. It will not be pushing correctly from its hind legs, and may be less than tidy with its front end. If the rider does this at a point where the horse is too far away to stand off, it may well put in an extra, unbalanced stride and refuse.

Left behind:

If the rider lacks confidence, or misjudges the moment of take-off and gets left behind, the weight on the horse's back will cause it to hollow and drop or cramp up its hind legs beneath it. There

Being very unconventional or unbalanced in your position can create real problems when tackling difficult combinations, larger fences, or when dealing with difficult horses. It is far better to try to adopt as classic a position as possible, which allows you to stay over the horse's centre of movement. Your stirrups will need to be shortened from normal flatwork length so that you are able to fold forward with your upper body, keeping the back flat and relaxed, and look ahead, while moving your seat backwards to act as a counterbalance. You can get a good feel of this by practising it standing on your own two feet. Here, Diane is demonstrating this position standing on a pole as though she were at the highest point of flight over a fence. Obviously this would be a rather exaggerated position over a smaller fence. Another useful exercise to develop balance, suppleness and security, is to ride in trot and canter in a similar squatting position with the seat raised slightly from the saddle, the joints flexed and acting as shock-absorbers, and avoiding using the rein contact for support.

is also a likelihood that unless the rider is quick-witted and secure enough to slip the reins, he will pull back on the horse's mouth, compounding its fright and anxiety.

Looking Down:

The rider's head is relatively heavy, and looking downwards will tend to collapse his ribcage and tip him forwards. In this position, he will be off balance, loose and insecure in the saddle, and lacking in effectiveness.

Leaning to One Side:

This fault is often accompanied by the rider's looking down to one side. It soon leads to the horse's becoming crooked and drifting to one side in the air, or to its having to twist its quarters awkwardly to one side in order to compensate for the loss of balance.

Legs

Locked Knees or Ankles:

The two often go together, and the inflexibility means that the joints cannot work as efficient shock-absorbers on landing and the lower leg becomes fixed and ineffective.

Standing in Stirrups:

If the rider stands in the stirrups instead of folding forwards from the hips, he will tend to get in front of the horse's movement and become unbalanced. In this position, he will need to use the horse's neck to support himself, which will restrict the horse with the reins as he does

Annette Miller has evolved a style all her own, which shows that even people with the most unorthodox of styles can still come out on top so long as they are consistent. Because she rides all her horses in the same way all the time they get used to it. However it would be very difficult for someone else to emulate this style so successfully, and it would not work for everyone anyway, so try to develop your own style.

This picture shows a rider achieving a clear round at a show by 'helping' an established showjumper to jump the front rail of a parallel – but this is not something that you should make a habit of doing with a young or less-experienced horse.

so. Very often he will also tend to pull back on the reins on take-off, which will lead to hollowness.

Toes Pointing Down:

This fault is often combined with knees gripping upwards. The rider will be lacking control of the lower legs, is likely to collapse forwards and will generally be lacking in security and more concerned with regaining his balance than in assisting the horse.

Lower Leg Too Far Back:

This may result from the rider standing up in the stirrups, but not always. Very sensitive horses may well object, while

the rider may be out of balance and in front of the movement on landing and unable to rebalance the horse and ride it forwards.

Lower Leg Too Far Forward:

This most frequently happens when the rider has got left behind, but it can happen if the heel has been forced downwards and forwards and become locked and rigid. This will make it difficult for him to stay with the horse over the fence.

Hands

Lifting Hands on Take-Off:

'Picking up' the horse on take-off with

Habitually trying to 'pick up' a horse with your hands – particularly if it is still learning its job – will cause it to hollow, as has happened in this picture. The rider is also standing up in her stirrups and using the rein contact for support, which is contributing to the problem. With a more independent seat, the rider would probably find it easier to trust the horse and resist the temptation to pick him up on take-off.

the reins will result in hollowing; riders who tend to stand in their stirrups are often guilty of it.

Lifting the Elbows:

If the elbows move upwards and outwards, although the rider may feel that he is giving the horse freedom of its head in the air, the reverse is true; the hands are more likely to be drawing back, restricting the headcarriage.

Dropping Contact on Take-Off:

A sudden loss of contact on take-off can unbalance the horse and cause it to lose confidence, prop itself on its forehand, put in a short, awkward stride, take off in a disorganized way, or refuse.

Restricting Hands:

Not following through in the air with the hands will restrict the movement of the head and neck, causing hollowness. If the rider is also restricting the horse on the approach it may well begin to fight the rider in order to escape the discomfort rather than concentrate on the fence.

Running Hands up Neck:

Although the rider is moving the hands forwards, the upwards direction of them will cause the horse to hollow. Hooking a thumb over the top of the neck will also be restricting and can lead to a dislocation or fracture of the digit.

Hooking Back with Contact:

Trying to hook the horse back to put it on to a stride, rather than riding forwards on to it will ultimately confuse and frustrate the horse. It often causes the horse to plunge on the last stride or two and make an inaccurate, hollow jump. Alternatively, it will inhibit the desire to go forward at all, and as it begins to lose impulsion it will jump awkwardly, make insufficient forward ground in the air or begin to refuse, even to rear. If a more collected gait is required, this must be achieved correctly, not by drawing the horse's front end in towards the rider.

Young or stuffy horses should be encouraged to continue in canter on landing after a fence. Here, Inky and Nina are both in good balance and moving forwards with impulsion and confidence.

FIRST FENCES

If a young horse appears a little hesitant initially, do not worry, it is usually a sign that it will, with careful training, be a careful jumper because it is wary of touching a pole. With this type of horse you need to be positive in sending it forwards – but without panicking or rushing it. If the horse does not go forward sufficiently, it will be even more inclined to 'balloon' its fences – jump very high and not make sufficient forward ground in the air – so it may well end up dropping its hind feet on to the fence on landing, which will make it increasingly anxious. If you find this happening, keep your fences very small for a while longer until the horse gains in

confidence and realizes that the pole is not going to leap up and bite.

On landing, it is easier, and natural, for the horse to continue in canter, even though the approach will have been from trot. Young and stuffy horses are best encouraged to continue in this gait for some strides after the fence to teach them to be forward thinking. Do not allow your horse to slop or hang back almost immediately on landing, no matter how pleased and relieved you may be to have safely negotiated it. Look ahead and ride forwards and straight for at least four or five strides so that it does not anticipate turning, and learns to move away from the fence with balance and impulsion. The way in which a horse leaves a fence is as important as the way it approaches it.

With an over-enthusiastic horse, or one that tends to become excitable, do not be afraid to mix flatwork with jumping; just because you have put a fence up does not mean that you have to keep jumping it. Spending some time in between fences, working in trot or even returning to walk, will do a lot to settle the horse, creating calmness and discipline. It may take time with some horses, but it is time well worth spending, particularly if you are reschooling and have returned to basics. If the horse does tend to rush on landing, be very careful how you go about steadying it again, as a severe reprimand with the reins is likely only to make matters worse (*see* Chapter 9, page 125). Gently but firmly steady the horse, trying to avoid pulling it off balance or causing it to hollow or back off the hand. It is early days, and a little tact and patience go a long way towards creating a good horse, or improving a difficult one. Remember, also, to change the rein frequently; it is all part of ensuring that neither you nor your horse becomes one-sided, as much as to prevent the horse from anticipating always turning in a certain direction, which could cause the horse to begin to drift a little in the air as a result.

Gradually introduce further single fences if you wish. A useful set up, which does not require a lot of equipment or effort to build, are three fences arranged in a Y shape. This allows a great deal of flexibility in that you can approach and ride away from them in any direction, and can also work around them with ease before deciding to approach another one. Because each of the three fences can be jumped from either side, it can do a lot to help reduce anticipation and is also very good practice for eventually jumping a

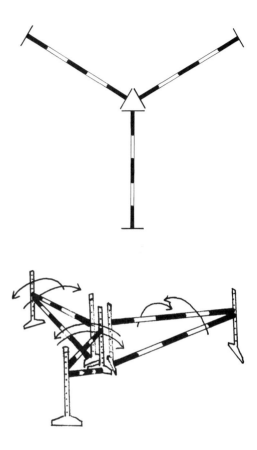

A Y-shaped arrangement of fences does not require a great deal of equipment but allows a lot of flexibility.

course as it encourages both horse and rider to maintain forwardness and fluency between fences.

SEEING A STRIDE

You will initially have been jumping out of trot, but if you have done your flatwork properly your horse will be able to canter correctly and calmly around corners and should be able to cope with approaching small obstacles from this gait. You are not, however, obliged to introduce the concept of cantering to a fence at this stage, and can if you prefer, leave it until later on when you bring in a second fence. Use your common sense and be guided by factors such as your horse's temperament and level of schooling. If you find that the horse begins to rush as a result of beginning to canter to fences, go back to pole work in trot and using placing poles again. Never be afraid to go back a few steps, repeat and re-establish earlier work if you begin to experience problems.

Provided the horse is staying confident, try to begin to 'see a stride' as early as possible in canter – that is, know roughly where your horse is going to take off, and be committed to riding positively to that point. It is, however, important to try to maintain the rhythm and length of stride rather than attempt to change it at the last minute in order to get the take-off precisely where you want it. Do not get your horse very short in canter and then fire it at the fence once you do see a stride, as it will only succeed in getting the horse worked up and anxious. Keep the horse balanced and rhythmical all the way to the fence; it will be able to jump far more easily and confidently like that, and will tire less quickly. It does take time and practice to be able to develop a really good eye for a stride, but always remember that you should be riding your horse forward on to it rather than hooking it back; the latter is likely to result in resistances, hollowness, excitability, loss of impulsion and a myriad of other problems.

Consistency in the stride you ride for is also very important. If it tends to be slightly long (and with most people it is) then stick to that; on the other hand, if you ride in very deep and close to a very correct take-off point, continue to do it. What you must not do is keep changing from long one moment to very deep the next, otherwise a young horse may become very uncertain and confused and will possibly begin refusing.

Some people do find it very difficult to 'see' a good stride (or even to see one at all) but it is largely a matter of practice and experience. If you find that you have met a fence wrongly and that, despite an otherwise good approach, the horse has got too close, or been forced to stand off or fit in an extra little short stride, try turning towards it the next time at a slightly different place. If the horse then meets it correctly, have someone on the ground mark the place you turned at so you can then judge the best place to ride your approach from each time thereafter. Alternatively, ask someone to put out a marker at the place where you have been seen to take three strides before meeting the fence, so that you know how far away you are each time and can learn to gauge it yourself. It does also help you to begin to see a better stride if you look at the bottom of the fence rather than at the top or back rail, as that is where you want the horse to take you, otherwise you will find yourself encouraging it to take off much too early.

INTRODUCING A SECOND FENCE

From jumping a single fence, the point at which you decide to introduce a second fence in a line with the first will be governed – again – by your own judgement and assessment of what you feel your horse's brain is ready for. There is no set time span for each stage – whether you are bringing on a youngster or going back to basics to resolve problems with an older horse – and you have to allow your instincts about how the horse is going and coping to guide you as to the right time to give it a little more to do. There are no short cuts if you want to do the job properly, though, and there is no point in spoiling it by trying to rush things along.

A horse has to be very quick-thinking for a double of fences and the first time through he may be taken a little by surprise if he is young and inexperienced. So even if you have progressed at this stage to jumping some slightly larger single fences, it is nevertheless a wise precaution to return to small fences – preferably cross-poles – so that height is not a problem. Even if the horse hangs back a little, with small fences it will be possible to keep the horse straight and encourage it to keep going forwards and hop over them. If you have done your pole work properly, it should not really pose too much of a problem.

Put a placing pole at a distance of about 9ft (2.7m) in front of the first fence (you will already have discovered the ideal distance for your horse) and then set up a second cross-pole at around 18–21ft (5.5–6.4m) beyond the first. This will allow the horse room to take one non-jumping stride in canter between the two fences. If the horse is a little spooky about the appearance of a second fence, and drops back into trot in front of it, do not hassle him immediately, although you should be positive and reassuring. Once the horse has popped over it a couple of times, it should quickly gain in confidence and be more prepared to go forwards. And remember that especially

if this is the first time the horse has been asked to canter on the approach to a fence, it will have a lot to think about.

If your horse is cantering happily enough on landing, but in a rather stuffy way and not really going forward enough, you can try putting a placing pole on the ground midway between the two fences to encourage it to take a more free-moving stride (having checked first, of course, that the distance between the two fences is one that is suitable for the horse's length of stride). Your horse may take a bit of a look at it the first time, so be prepared to maintain impulsion and keep the horse going forward. With this type of horse it can be tempting to try to create more impetus on landing by cantering into the first fence, but it is on the whole best to stick to approaching from trot over a placing pole set at an appropriate distance. With both stuffy and onward-bound horses – whether you are dealing with a simple or more complex grid – you will gain much more from an approach to the first fence in trot as it will help to develop a more athletic jump right from the start. It will also help to ensure that succeeding fences are met more correctly (as there will be less inclination to stand off or jump in too boldly), and it will develop his concentration, balance and ability to think quickly once in the middle of a combination.

As your horse grows in confidence, you can go on to introduce a spread fence as the second fence. Probably the safest way of doing this is to build an ascending spread of some kind so that the back rail is easily visible. Eventually you can build it up into a true parallel with both top poles at the same height, which will really encourage the horse to

A cross-pole is a useful schooling fence which encourages a straight approach. There is no reason why cross-poles cannot be built in the form of spreads as well as uprights.

use its back end freely and 'open up' a little in the air.

When you start cantering into a spread fence (or a second fence for that matter) do be careful not to fall into the trap of over-riding your horse just because it is wider. You do want impulsion, but this is true of any fence, and at all costs you do want to avoid increasing the speed (particularly with excitable horses) as it will lead rapidly to rushing, hollowness and inaccurate jumping – all those things that are so undesirable.

Again, as you feel your horse is ready, build a third fence – another cross-pole – at a distance of approximately 6.4–7.6m (21–25ft). This will help to keep the horse central through the line and, being a vertical, will encourage it to pick itself up, engage its hocks and rebalance itself on landing after the spread rather than landing in a heap or running on to its forehand.

Be constructive in your work, and do not lose sight of the fact that gridwork is a means to an end – not an end in itself. Your aim is to progress on from this stage by taking note of what your horse is doing and by selecting types of fence and distances that are going to produce the best result or improvement. Insert cross-poles, verticals and spreads where they will be of benefit – not just for the sake of it.

8 Developing Gridwork Exercises

Grids can be made easier or more demanding as you wish, but do gear them to your horse's experience and ability; there is nothing to be gained from asking a horse to do something it is not ready for or simply is not capable of. Your fences do not need to be big, although the occasional slightly larger fence will help to keep a horse from becoming complacent. Remember that you are not using gridwork to find out how high the horse can get off the ground, but rather to teach it how to jump in a good shape, to approach fences confidently, straight, and without changing rhythm, losing balance or impulsion, and as much as possible to be clever, careful and quick thinking. In other words, the purpose of gridwork is to educate a horse so that, if it has the inherent ability to go on and jump bigger fences in competition, it will be in the strongest possible position to utilize that ability to the full.

Do not forget, either, that the size, type, conformation or temperament of some horses is not ideally suited to a discipline that requires accuracy and athleticism, and that these characteristics are by and large unalterable. While boldness and courage are an asset, they are not sufficient on their own, and sometimes you will need to compromise. This is especially true of gridwork, when to get the most benefit from it you need to be observant and aware of your horse's shortcomings so that you can set suitable exercises. However, a lot of the challenge and fascination of training your horse more often than not lies in trying to find a satisfactory solution to difficulties posed by these factors – it is often more satisfying to get a good tune out of a difficult horse than it is to make faster progress with an easier one. Although it may take longer and you may have to work harder to succeed, you are likely to learn a great deal more in the process.

Generally speaking, vertical fences and tighter distances will encourage your horse to be quicker and tidier in front and to stay in a nice round shape. Horses

Do not forget to praise your horse when it makes a good effort. Even if it has had a fence down, it may have been trying hard for you, and it is important to recognize and reward this.

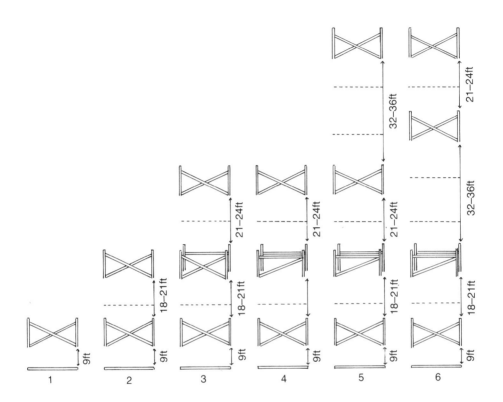

This is one way in which a simple grid can be built up into a more demanding exercise. Dotted lines between fences indicate where poles may be placed on the ground if necessary to encourage the correct number of strides. Exercises 1–4 have already been discussed in Chapter 7 (see page 101); one way of progressing on from this point is to introduce a fourth fence in the line, with two non-jumping strides after the third fence. This will encourage a slightly stuffy horse to continue to go forwards and help to maintain impulsion, which can sometimes be lost when riding over several fences with only one non-jumping stride between each. Alternatively, you might try using exercise 6 with a horse that tends to run on to its forehand when asked to take more than one non-jumping stride. The last two vertical fences will help encourage the horse to engage its hocks and lighten its forehand again. This exercise will also get a horse to think more quickly and can be useful with an impetuous animal. Of course this is only one example of the way in which you can adapt a grid to serve your purposes: with common sense, observation and a little thought, you can work out the most beneficial combination of fences, distances and placing poles to improve your horse or help sort out the problems you have when competing.

that tend to be stuffy or have poor technique behind will usually benefit more from using spread fences in grids. You should, however, bear in mind that if you are working over tighter distances it will be far more difficult for your horse to jump from a parallel to a parallel than for it to cope with a vertical to a parallel or a parallel to a vertical. So do set your problems fairly and within your horse's

Points to Remember when Tackling Gridwork

• Do approach as straight as possible. Using cross-poles will help to keep your horse straight. They do not necessarily have to be very small – they can be built to about 90cm (3ft) in the centres.

• Do look ahead, not down at the ground, as this will unbalance both horse and rider and can affect the length of stride, which makes a 'correct' distance for your horse wrong.

• Do keep your leg on – without over-riding – to maintain impulsion through an exercise.

• Don't collapse between fences or at the end of a grid; it will unbalance the horse, putting it on to its forehand with a loss of impulsion and inability to bring its hocks beneath it again ready for the next stride or fence.

• Don't allow your upper body to fold forward to one side as this will encourage the horse to drift and become crooked to the next fence.

• Know your horse – when to ask for more, when it is doing its best, and when to call it a day. Do try to end on a good note, and do praise the horse when it has made a good effort. Don't forget that your horse may have made a good effort even if it had a pole or two down.

• Don't start straight away with a grid of several fences. Start with a single jump and add each additional element bit by bit so as to maintain confidence. How quickly you introduce each successive fence depends upon the experience of the horse, the nature of any problems it has, and how it is going on that particular day. Be prepared to be flexible and play it by ear.

• If an exercise is not achieving the result you want, do change it in some way to preserve interest, confidence and to be more constructive, rather than persevere with it, otherwise you are likely to create problems.

• If your horse meets the first fence of a grid correctly and jumps it well, take care not to over-ride and chase it into successive fences. Sit quietly and do only what is necessary in terms of keeping it between hand and leg and moving with impulsion.

• Suggested distances given in Chapter 6 are just that – suggestions – and you do not need to adhere rigidly to them. Vary them to suit your horse's requirements, but don't be over-enthusiastic with this, as a change in distance of just 15cm (6in) can make a big difference.

ability: the aim is always to educate, never to trap.

Try not to have more than four fences in a grid. Although you can have five, or even six, four fences nevertheless asks for a tremendous amount of effort from the horse (especially if it is a youngster) and you can produce the results you want just as easily with fewer fences as with more. It is also important to preserve

Placing poles can help to bring the horse to a more correct take-off point, but take care when dealing with horses that tend to stand off their fences habitually in case they try to take off from in front of the pole instead of stepping over it. Here, the pole is drawn out quite a distance so that Inky is able to take off from his usual point and there is no temptation for him to take off earlier still; the whole impression here is of his throwing himself towards the jump instead of pushing himself over it with his hocks beneath him, and he is not folding his front legs back at all.

balance, rhythm, and impulsion at all times, and sometimes using a simpler grid will develop or restore this far better than a more complex combination.

When jumping through a grid, do try to have a very soft, yielding contact, allowing the horse to find its own way through it. If the horse feels wrong, or hits a pole, do not panic; resist the temptation to interfere, other than in keeping the horse going forward. The next time through it will have learnt from its error. It is a mistake to try to put a horse right

and help it too much. It will learn a far more lasting lesson by being allowed to work it out for itself. In addition, trying to correct a horse in the middle of a grid is not only more likely to distract it from the job in hand than to assist it, but to encourage it to become increasingly reliant on its rider instead of learning to be more clever. Worse still, if you actually make a mistake in judgement, the horse's confidence in you will be shaken or even completely shattered. As the horse becomes more confident, it can

Once his stepping over the pole is established, it is drawn slightly closer towards the fence.

Finally, the pole has been moved in closer still, which brings him to a far better take-off point. The placing pole is now almost the same distance away from the fence as the point he was originally taking off from, which shows just how far he was standing off. You can see how much more athletically he is using his hocks now, really bringing them forward underneath himself rather than flinging himself forward.

in fact be a very good exercise to allow the rein contact to become quite loose once you have got into a grid, staying in a balanced forward position with your weight over your knees so that the horse is allowed to make all the effort and to concentrate with the minimum of interference or distraction. It will learn very quickly to balance itself and use its head and neck freely to assist itself. Obviously you do sometimes get occasions when a horse will start to take advantage and run out, but that is something which you will have to deal with if and when it crops up (*see* Chapter 9, page 125).

BOUNCE FENCES

A 'bounce' fence (where there is no non-jumping stride within a grid) can be very beneficial as it will encourage quick-thinking and agility in your horse and will help to make it more supple in its back. It is best to keep bounce fences at the beginning of a grid rather than in the middle or at the end, as there is a danger that the horse may otherwise mistake it and try to take it on as a spread. With horses that are overconfident or prone to overjumping, it is probably wise to leave bounce fences until they are more experienced and settled. Even if you do succeed – by lengthening the distance considerably – in obtaining a 'bounce' with this type of horse, it can result in its attempting to 'bounce' one-stride combinations – so proceed with caution.

Bounce fences are not always very successful with stuffy horses, either, as they do not encourage sufficient forward movement. Very stiff-backed horses will also find them very difficult to cope with, so they should be used with great care. Making a horse uncomfortable will not improve its confidence or attitude.

Whatever the type of horse, bounce fences are very hard work, so they do not need to be made very big. The first part should be used more like a raised placing pole if anything, just high enough to create a jump. The second element of a bounce should always be a vertical, never a parallel. While you may see horses tackling this sort of problem at the big cross-country events, you must remember that you are watching very experienced, very talented and very athletic horses in action.

LANDING POLES

Grids are basically combinations of fences, so if you have problems at shows you can improve your combination jumping at home. If you find that your horse is not making sufficient ground between fences, set up a double or treble at the distance you are having trouble with, and place a pole on the ground midway between them. Provided you keep your leg on, your horse will land and then jump the pole, which will extend his stride so that he then arrives at the right take-off point for the next fence. You can also do the same for combinations with two or three strides between each element, using a pole for each stride.

Similarly, poles on the ground can be of help with a horse that tends to jump into a fence too boldly, landing too far out beyond it. Here, the pole will help to teach the horse to shorten itself again. Horses that tend to become a little bit too quick through grids, especially when the fences are larger, do need impulsion,

Pat and Friday tackling a bounce fence. Although she is resting her hands on Friday's neck, Pat is in a good, secure and effective position and is allowing the mare plenty of rein so that she can use her head and neck freely.

Friday often tends to move on to her forehand and fade away after a fence. A pole is put on the ground just beyond the fence, and the first time through she takes a good look at it and hangs a little to the left, hoping to avoid it; the jump wings on each side encourage her not to duck out but to hop over the pole instead.

The second time through produces a much better effort. Pat has also taken the precaution of transferring her whip to her left hand, and knowing what to expect, Friday takes a little jump over it, having to engage her hocks to do so and thus helping to lift her forehand and propel herself forward for the next stride. It would also help a lot if Pat's upper body was less forward over Friday's shoulders at this stage.

A pole on the ground can also be used to help establish the correct canter lead after a single fence or grid by placing it at an angle in the next corner. Darcy frequently tends to land on the right canter lead. After riding through the exercises shown in the diagram several times, he was still consistently landing in right canter, but whenever Stewart asked him to turn to the left he began automatically to produce a neat flying change through the corner rather than attempting to negotiate it as previously on the wrong leg.

(a)

(b)

(c)

(d)

but you do not want them to become habitually faster and flatter when you put your leg on; poles on the floor can again sometimes prove to be of assistance because as the horse lands, it will have to think, drop its head and look for the pole, and that should help slow it down. Do take care not to place landing poles too close to the final element of a grid or single fence, however.

With experience, you can begin to develop your gridwork, using not just different types of fences, but distances between them to make your horse more elastic and quick-thinking, moving from a shorter distance to one where he will have to lengthen, and back to a shortened distance again. As before, use poles on the ground to help initially rather than resort to acrobatics in the saddle to try to induce the horse to lengthen, or severe rein aids to shorten it. Obviously, some work on the flat is a good preparation, too.

One other problem that ground poles can help to solve is a tendency to land after a grid on the wrong canter lead, or disunited. Rather than stopping and correcting the horse each time it happens, place a pole in the next corner at an angle of about 45 degrees, and continue in canter. As you reach the pole ask the horse for a little pop over it and put the horse right. With repetition the horse will soon learn to balance and correct itself, and will develop the co-ordination to produce flying changes voluntarily when riding a change of direction while jumping a course of fences.

When schooling over fences, attitude is all-important. Keep your horse interested and do not bore it with endless and unnecessary repetition. If possible, take the horse through a grid a couple of times and then give it an extended canter or two before returning to the grid again. If you have asked the horse to jump a couple of bigger fences, always jump another smaller, simple obstacle before finishing your lesson to ensure that you finish on a note of confidence. If the horse has had to make a huge effort it is easy for it to be a little frightened by the experience, and popping over a small fence is good insurance against any little doubts it might have in its mind as a result.

Finally, bear in mind that whatever you build by way of a grid, it should serve a purpose and be used to obtain improvement. Decide just what you want to achieve with your horse and choose those fences and distances most likely to help you to obtain those aims.

9 Troubleshooting

No horse is perfect, and it is inevitable that at some point you will encounter problems of some kind. While this chapter deals with the most common, obviously it is not an exhaustive guide. Sometimes problems are not entirely straightforward to assess in terms of cause and remedy, because often there is not just one, but several contributing factors. If you do have a problem, never be afraid to ask for help from an experienced person; quite often someone on the ground is actually in a better position to see the source of the trouble than you are in the saddle.

BUCKING ON LANDING

This can be an unnerving (and unseating) experience for the rider caught unawares. It can sometimes be caused simply by high spirits, in which case the problem will disappear as the horse settles down to serious work. However, it is all too easy for misbehaviour arising from exuberance to develop into an established habit, so if the horse is a little overfresh for some reason it is common sense to spend sufficient time working on the flat prior to jumping. This will ensure that

If you do encounter a problem do not be afraid to ask for help from an experienced person who may sometimes find it easier to spot the source of the problem from the ground than you can from the saddle. It never hurts to have someone check on you from time to time anyway as sometimes your horse can feel very good but in reality look diabolical!

Bucking after a Fence

Before exploring other possible causes, check that the horse is not reacting to discomfort. Factors that can cause discomfort include:
- Incorrectly fitted or adjusted saddlery.
- Insensitive riding, such as landing heavily on the horse's back.
- The rider adopting an unbalanced position in the saddle.
- Back pain.

---

the horse is settled and obedient. It may also be worth looking at the food-to-work ratio, as a lot of riders are often guilty of overfeeding for the amount of work the horse is doing

Bucking after a fence may also be caused by the horse feeling a twinge in its back, especially if it has made a particularly athletic jump over a large or demanding obstacle. However, some horses can be a little bloody-minded and, provided physical problems can be ruled out as a cause, it often helps on landing to be ready to send the horse forward into the bridle, riding it on to a circle or even to another fence. By giving the horse a little more to think about and requiring it to engage its hocks, it will make it far less inclined to buck, as well as making it physically far more difficult. Hanging on to the rein contact in anticipation of a buck will often aggravate the problem as it allows the horse to lose forward momentum and prop on to its forehand; a contact is essential, but it should not be a restrictive one.

Nine times out of ten, though, bucking after a fence usually indicates discomfort of some kind, so it is essential that the saddle is examined for correct fit, and the back and mouth checked. Jumping will often aggravate back problems and, if this is the case, it may be noticeable that the horse is also jumping very hollow. Discomfort can also be caused if the rider gets left behind, sits up too early, or lands heavily on the horse's back. It does not take long for the horse to begin to anticipate the pain and try to rid itself of the source. It is also worth checking on your lower leg position as some horses will object strenuously if it slips back too far. Apart from any other considerations, it is neither a safe nor effective position to be in and, since it will result in tipping the rider forwards, it will also adversely affect the horse's balance.

CARELESSNESS

Generally, most horses do not like hitting fences, but some are naturally more careful than others, and these are the ones who will make the best – and safest – showjumpers in the long run. Unfortunately, there is no way in which you can teach a horse that really does not care about hitting its fences to be more careful, although luckily they are in the minority. They can be frustrating in that one day they will come out of the stable

A horse that is careless over show jumps will often turn out to have more respect for solid fences and will make a good hunter or cross-country horse instead.

INCONSISTENCY

Inconsistency is more often caused by the rider than the horse: inconsistent horses are the product of inconsistent riding. Faced with this problem, it is worth going back to basics, working on the flat to try to develop a more regular rhythm, length of stride and balance, and using placing poles to encourage a more accurate approach and take-off, and to teach the rider to develop a better eye for a stride. Repetition and practice are the answer, although the horse must never be allowed to become bored.

Similarly, 'four faultitis' in competition is usually the fault of the rider, often occurring at the first or last fence when jumping a course or, indeed at a fence which the rider is apprehensive about. At these fences the rider may try to

minority. They can be frustrating in that one day they will come out of the stable feeling like a million dollars and jump beautifully, but on another they will have reverted and just will not be bothered to make the effort. However, quite often this sort of horse will make a good hunter: while it may be careless when showjumping it has a healthy respect for the solid, unyielding quality of natural fences.

There can be reasons other than temperament for carelessness, such as boredom, not being able to cope with the height or width, insufficient impulsion, or even that the horse is too busy fighting the rider to concentrate fully on the job in hand, but these should all be immediately apparent to the rider and the solutions are obvious.

'Four faultitis.'

approach too carefully, trying too hard, becoming anxious and over-riding the horse. Having knocked the fence down as a result, the rider will then often relax and jump any remaining fences beautifully! It is easy to let the pressure of competition and the desire to do well get to you and affect your riding, but the more you do the less nerves will affect you, and the easier it will be to relax and allow the horse to give of its best as you would do at home.

SPOOKINESS

Spooky horses often make the best showjumpers because they tend to be naturally more careful. They will back off their fences and drop their heads on the approach to see what they are doing and, when they actually get to the fence, they will often jump that little bit bigger than most.

It is important to be patient and not to rush this sort of horse if it is to remain confident. Rather than sticking to the same sort of fence all the time, or increasing the height, encourage the horse to go forwards and broaden its experience of as many different types of fence as possible. Give your own jumps a lick of fresh paint, hire or borrow fences so it can be introduced to filler boards, water trays, planks, and so on, and let it see as many varied obstacles as possible. Shows that run clear-round classes are often a good place to take youngsters as the fences are rarely high enough to present a problem but they will be unfamiliar. Since it is not judged as a proper competition, there is no time limit and if you have a couple of stops you are normally allowed to continue rather than having to leave the ring.

STRONG PULLING

As with so many jumping problems, before trying anything else it is vital that physical causes can be ruled out. In the case of a horse that pulls strongly, check the mouth for signs of sharp teeth, ulcers, gum disorders, and so on. Although it is possible to check the front of the mouth and first molars yourself, it is best to get a vet to check that a problem does not exist further back along the jaws, which can only be done properly using a special gag. After physical discomfort is eliminated, you should also consider other causes, such as insufficient schooling. It may well be that further schooling is needed in order to encourage better acceptance of hand and leg.

Although you want your horse to be taking you to the fence, and taking a feel forward on the bit, you do not want it to become overstrong to the point where you are unable to balance and adjust the horse when necessary, and where it becomes a constant battle to retain even a modicum of control. Having to haul constantly at the horse's mouth is not only exhausting for the rider, but painful and sometimes frightening for the horse, and may cause it to fight more, not less, against the contact. It is ultimately much kinder to upgrade the bit to something that the horse has more respect for, and that can be used more sympathetically, than to persevere with a milder one.

It may be necessary to experiment a little with different bits in order to find the most suitable one (*see* Chapter 3). With a horse that tends to be strong, but also overbends and tucks its chin in against its chest to evade the influence of the bit, experimentation with bits may provide a partial solution to the problem (those that employ curb chains are usually less successful). But the rider should also put more leg on to push the horse forward on to the contact and use frequent half-halts rather than resort to a constant backwards tension on the reins, which can soon teach it to drop behind the bit, or make it worse if it already does this.

Horses that rake down at the bit usually do so because they are uncomfortable. Apart from checking for physical problems and ensuring that the rider is not being rather heavy-handed, it may again be necessary to try a number of different bits until you find something in which you know you can hold the horse easily, but to which the horse does not object. In order for a bit to do its job effectively, it may also be necessary to select a different type of noseband to use in conjunction with it.

REFUSING AT SHOWS

The horse that jumps well at home but stops when at shows (even though it may have been working well in the collecting ring) creates a lot of frustration for the rider, although often the blame for this can be laid at his door. When jumping at home the horse is, of course, on familiar territory, with familiar fences, and knows very well that if it misbehaves it can expect a reprimand. Some of the problem can also be down to lack of experience, in which case take the horse to lots of little shows, hire the facilities at an equestrian centre, or take the horse over to a friend's yard to school over different fences in a different place. Keep

the jumps very small and give it some education and new experiences. After all, it is no good being able to jump 4ft 6in at home over a simple upright if you cannot get over a 2ft plank elsewhere!

Sometimes the problem is caused by what has been happening in the collecting ring: for instance, insufficient working in to ensure concentration and collection between hand and leg (particularly in an exciting atmosphere where there are lots of distractions), or, more frequently, overdoing things. If you have jumped the practice fence twenty or thirty times while waiting for your turn, the horse is going to be tired and may decide that he has had enough by the time you go into the ring. You should not really need to jump more than three or four uprights and a couple of spread fences before going into the ring – you are only supposed to be loosening the horse off, not indulging in a major training session. Take care not to overdo the amount of jumping at shows either; four rounds (two first rounds and two jump-off rounds) are sufficient, otherwise you will end up sickening the horse.

Rider nerves can also contribute to the problem. You may actually be riding quite well out in the collecting ring, but once you go into the main ring – especially if you are inexperienced – and feel attention focused on you, your riding may deteriorate. If you suddenly become anxious, ineffective and passive, or alternatively over-ride the horse, it can destroy the horse's confidence. Be positive by all means, but do not overdo it to the point where you actively interfere and make it impossible for the horse to co-operate. If you do suffer from nerves to this extent, the answer is simply to do more competition work over small clear-round fences until you get over your stage fright and can worry more about what the horse is doing and less about who is watching you.

Of course, some horses – and there are always a few – are clever and know that when you are in the ring in front of judges they cannot be reprimanded. This is a difficult situation. The only thing you can really do is to set up a false 'show' at a friend's place, get lots of friends and their horses round, build a course and make it all as realistic as possible. Then, if you do have to reprimand your horse, adjust fences or whatever, at least you can do so without having to worry about the judges, or having to leave the ring through elimination – with the horse learning that it cannot get away with it.

HOLLOWING

The horse that jumps 'hollow' (with an inverted topline) will make a shallow arc across a fence, with its back concave and head carried high. This may be accompanied by a tendency to allow the forelimbs to dangle, and because the head is not lowered the hindquarters will not be drawn upwards and forwards, but will trail. In order to clear a fence with this flat arc, the horse will need to stand off, because if it does meet it at a more correct, closer take-off point, it will roll the pole with its front legs on the way up. Back problems, ill-fitting saddlery, or the rider's getting left behind, can all be responsible for hollowness and need to be investigated as possible sources of the trouble. Especially where young horses are concerned, if the rider has got left behind and landed heavily in the

saddle, or inadvertently taken a pull on its mouth in the air, it is enough to frighten it into going hollow, even if it has been going well up to that point. It is important to realize when this has happened and to go back a couple of stages for at least a day or two. Horses that tend to be a bit faint-hearted and do not perhaps enjoy their jumping may also tend to jump hollow, particularly as fences grow larger and more demanding, so you do need to know your horse and just how much it is fair to ask of it. A horse that is lacking in confidence for some reason is not a particularly safe ride and will ultimately injure either itself or its rider.

Provided the horse's training has been started correctly with flatwork, and fences encouraging roundness and athleticism, it should continue its show-jumping career that way. However, if you have a horse that despite good beginnings does jump hollow, do not necessarily write it off, as some very good international horses have exhibited the same trait (although good horses that jump hollow do tend to be rare). It is possible to improve it to a certain extent, but it will take a long time if the horse has been allowed to work in this manner for a few years, since it will not only be lacking the desirable musculature along the topline, but is also likely to have built up the opposing muscles (such as those on the underside of the neck). To 'lose' them and build up the right ones does take many, many months of work. Obviously the horse must be worked correctly on the flat, while using placing poles and parallels in small grids. Slowly tightening up distances will teach the horse to take off close to the fence and, provided the rider allows plenty of

Occasionally you have to ask a horse a question, as happened here. This is a jump-off against the clock. Ross was interfering on the approach but, having done so, he did give the horse plenty of freedom in the rein contact in the air. Nevertheless it resulted in his inadvertently causing the horse to hollow in the air. Owing to good preparation and training, he was able to make a good recovery on landing, turning to the left and inside the caravan in the background, and succeeded in winning the class. Although it is not something you would want to do when schooling at home – as it will teach the horse very quickly to become hollow as a matter of habit – sometimes you have to take a gamble when competing in order to win. (Photo courtesy of MVR Photographic.)

freedom in the head and neck, encourage it to use itself in a rounder and more athletic way.

Whether you decide that this course of action is worth pursuing depends to an extent upon the age of the horse. With a youngster it is probably worth the time and effort involved, but if you have an older horse who has been jumping like this for some time you may never be

entirely successful and may in fact create more problems than you solve by attempting to change it so radically. Provided you do not encourage the horse to stand off its fences progressively further and further away and as long as it is coping adequately it can sometimes be the wiser policy to leave well alone.

In this sequence, Oz is moving crookedly on his approach to the fence and Jackie is attempting to correct and straighten him, with her hands. She is achieving only partial success: by the time Oz arrives at the fence he is still crooked in his presentation to it and has neither the impulsion or confidence to jump it, so he refuses.

This was a much better approach. Jackie has used her legs to keep Oz going forward and straight rather than relying entirely on the rein contact. As a result, he is better able to tackle the fence and looks confident and happy about it. Jackie is leaning a little to the left, which is probably why he is jumping a little crookedly still rather than meeting the fence in the middle.

inside rein to try to correct the approach will restrict the forward movement on that side and make the horse inclined to crab sideways. Try instead to maintain a more equal contact on both reins, preventing any excessive bend in the neck, and use more leg to straighten the horse: if it is swinging its body to the left, for example, use more left leg. If you have upgraded the flatwork, the horse will understand what you are asking it to do, and you will also have learnt how to react in the correct manner to this problem.

QUARTERS TWISTING IN FLIGHT

This problem may arise because the horse has made an awkward jump or has not made enough forward ground in the

CROOKED APPROACH

Sometimes a young horse will snake a little on the approach to a fence; this is usually a result of greenness. The problem can also arise with gassier types of horses that rush if the rider is attempting to take control entirely from the front end and with insufficient leg. As with many jumping problems, this one involves going back to basics on the flat. If you cannot get the horse to work between hand and leg and it is insufficiently schooled to respond to and move away from the increased pressure of either leg, you are never going to be able to approach a fence correctly anyway.

Having remedied this state of affairs, when approaching a fence it is important to use your legs rather than your hands to counteract any tendency to move crookedly towards it. Pulling on the

The mare has twisted her quarters to one side considerably – you can see her off hind just to the side of the rider's foot. It is not something that she does normally, and it most likely happened on this occasion because the rider collapsed to one side, becoming very crooked and causing the mare to compensate for the loss of balance.

133

air (particularly over a spread) but if it is a regular occurrence it may well be caused by physical discomfort, and the horse should be checked over by a vet.

It does also sometimes happen because the rider has dropped to either the left or right over the horse's shoulder so that it has to compensate its balance by twisting its quarters to the side in the air.

LACK OF IMPULSION AFTER A FENCE

Sometimes you will find that a horse wants to move away from a fence very slowly. This creates problems when riding through a combination of fences as you will not be able to gain enough ground between them for a correct take-off. It can also be very jarring on the horse's fore legs if it continually jumps like this, and the resultant discomfort can make it even less inclined to move freely away from a fence.

You will need to be very positive in this situation, setting up a small fence and approaching it at a very strong canter. Wear a pair of spurs if necessary, carry a stick and, if needed, give the horse a sharp smack with it behind the girth (having first taken that hand off the reins), to send the horse forward. Although it may sound harsh, it is ultimately for the horse's good, and if it is moderately intelligent it will soon realize what is expected of it.

It is not always the horse who is to blame. Many novice and amateur riders are often so relieved to have cleared a fence that they simply are not thinking about the next one and riding the horse forward to it. Once you have taken off at a fence, it is history, and although you

can be pleased at having jumped it you must have your mind fixed on the next one. If you do find that you tend to land in a heap, keep your fences small and simply come round and do it again and again until you get it right. The way in which you leave your fences is as important as the way in which you approach them.

NOT GOING FORWARD SUFFICIENTLY TO FENCES

There may be a very simple reason for this happening. For instance, if the fence is sited so that the horse is being asked to jump it going away from the entrance/exit of your working area, or away from the collecting ring at a show, it may be inclined to hang back. While this may be an understandable reason, it does not make it any more forgivable, and if it is not dealt with firmly the problem will become worse. The horse should be ridden forward positively into the contact and you should insist that it moves forwards from the leg at all times (*see* Chapter 4). Impulsion needs to be established from the start, rather than trying to create it at the last minute when it is too late.

If it happens consistently and regardless of the fences' siting, there could well be a physical problem at the root of it. Or it may be that the horse has simply not learnt to move forwards from leg into hand, or it may be that it is over-bitted. Hard ground can make a normally fluent horse rather sticky. With a horse that is generally rather stuffy, however, your riding needs to be positive, and in fact gridwork can prove very

Nina has used her stick to encourage Rosie to be more positive and forward-going over the placing pole in front of the fence; the stick should really be used more directly behind the leg. Nina has also come behind the movement and her rein contact is rather restrictive – both these factors have caused the mare to hollow and lose co-ordination. Take care with the sort of horse you do this with. It may be successful with some, but with others it may be better to return to flatwork to encourage a better response to the leg. You can see here how Rosie has become so distracted by what Nina is doing that she is not really concentrating on the fence in front of her.

beneficial with this sort of animal. Keep the fences fairly small so that they are well within the horse's ability, start with the distances between them fairly short and gradually lengthen them out. If it is inclined to fade away, it often helps to put a pole on the ground midway between each fence so that the horse is encouraged to step forward over it and on to the next fence. Try to avoid making the common mistake of throwing the front end away; even though it feels as though you are doing the wrong thing and slowing the horse down still further you must have a positive contact. If there is no contact for the horse to go into, it will be unbalanced and, no matter how much leg you use, it will be unable to engage its hocks beneath it in order to propel itself forwards to the fence.

RUSHING

Horses that rush their fences are usually inaccurate jumpers, flat or hollowed in shape, and often inclined to stand off their fences as well. Such a style of approach can not only be hair-raising for the rider, but also very unsafe. It is a commonly encountered problem. Most people assume that because the horse is taking its fences at speed it must be enthusiastic and enjoying itself, but more frequently, it is in reality caused by a lack of confidence or even fear. A horse that is sensitive and eager to please may continue to jump, even when it is afraid; rather than stop, it will increase its speed to try to get the job over and done with as quickly as possible. With such horses, it is wise to try to analyse the source of the anxiety in order to restore confidence. It may, for example, stem from the rider's getting left behind, a jab in the mouth or being restricted with the contact in the air. It does not take long for a horse to begin to anticipate the worst once it has happened a couple of times. Physical problems can also be to blame: if the horse is in pain from its mouth, back, or from badly fitting saddlery, it will be inclined to run away and try to escape the discomfort.

Riders can also be responsible for causing a rushing problem, often without being aware of having done so. If there has been a problem such as the horse stopping once or twice, the rider may well anticipate it happening again. This will lead him to ride the horse forward over-strongly to prevent it; the horse becomes quicker and quicker as a result and, while the rider thinks he is doing the right thing, the horse is in fact probably losing confidence rather than gaining it. It is often beneficial to return to basics, spending time achieving a better rapport and settling the horse. Polework can also be of tremendous help before returning to jumping work that is designed to increase confidence: keep the fences small and simple initially. If the horse does become anxious and hurried, be patient and take care not to over-correct it as this may have been the source of the problem in the first place. Anticipation of a severe reprimand via the bit may only make matters worse, and bullying tactics are best avoided.

Some people are greatly in favour of loose jumping to help restore confidence in a horse that rushes, and do in fact get a lot out of it, but it depends on whether you have the facilities for this, and to an extent upon trial and error, since what works for one horse does not necessarily help another. Some horses do in fact feel a little abandoned when left without any guidance whatsoever, in which case lungeing may be more beneficial. It should go without saying that whoever does the lungeing needs to be really competent at it for the horse to gain any benefit.

When considering the problem of

Common Causes of Rushing

- Natural sharpness.
- Lack of confidence, or fear.
- Physical pain, often in the mouth or back.
- Discomfort caused by ill-fitting saddlery.
- Over-strong riding.
- Anticipation of severe reprimand.

Lungeing over fences is sometimes instructive in that it gives you the opportunity to see what the horse is doing over its fences, but you do need to be very proficient in order to do this successfully. Here, the pony has had its head pulled to the inside of the circle, which in turn has made it twist its body to the side, which is why its forelegs are not level. Because the lunge rein has been thrown up in the air to prevent it from catching on the wings it has also distracted the pony's attention away from the fence. Ideally a plank or piece of semi-rounded fencing leaned on the inside wing would allow the lunge rein to slide freely up it without catching and would prevent interference in this way. If the jump had been positioned against the outside wall of the school it would also have meant that the trainer would not have needed to use the lunge rein to keep the pony straight.

rushing, much depends upon the temperament of the horse. While a large proportion rush because they are afraid, others are not so much worried as naturally very sharp. There are several ways of approaching the problem with this sort of horse; be prepared to experiment to find out which works best. Riding a number of circles in front of a fence and only jumping it when the horse is settled and has ceased to anticipate it may help, although it will take a lot of time, patience and quiet riding in order to begin to see some improvement. It is important that when doing this, the rider remains quiet on leaving the circle and approaching the fence, and resists the temptation to chase the horse into it the last few strides. The rider must also resist the temptation to have a continual backwards tension on the reins, which will encourage the horse to run on even more.

Another method of dealing with this type of horse is using gridwork, as it does give it something to think about,

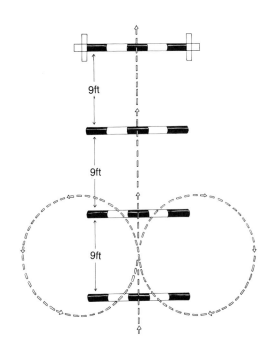

9ft

9ft

9ft

This is a useful exercise for a horse that rushes. It combines the discipline and accuracy of one of the earlier trotting-pole exercises (detailed in Chapter 5) with a small fence.

although, equally, it can sometimes make a horse even quicker instead. Try building two fences at a distance of approximately 13.7–14.6m (45–48ft), to allow three non-jumping strides, and allow the horse to jump it once. As usual, it will probably quicken up and possibly even knock down the second part as a result. Then raise the height of the second fence – not by one or two holes, but by 30–60cm (1–2ft) – and allow the horse to come round into it again. It is quite likely that the horse will again hit it hard, but if it is at all careful it will have learnt from the mistake and the next time round will begin to steady itself and back off instead.

Often you will find that the more boldly a fence is built – using brightly coloured filler boards or even a couple of Bloks – the more it will help to encourage the horse to slow down and back off. Some people will throw a rug or a jacket over a fence to make it more spooky and to produce much the same result, but you should be aware that this practice is not allowed at BSJA affiliated shows.

Backing Off

The term 'backing off' is not always correctly understood. It does not mean that the horse has lost impulsion, rhythm or balance and, as a result, props in front of the fence with its front legs (followed in most cases by an awkward stride and equally awkward jump). Rather, it means that the horse has learnt to adjust its stride before a fence with no loss of balance, rhythm or impulsion, drawing its hocks well forward beneath it (instead of falling on to its forehand), and is thus able to jump more cleanly, powerfully, with a better shape and, provided that the horse is between hand and leg, without much help from the rider. When doing this, the horse gives the impression that it is sitting back on its hocks away from the fence.

REFUSING

This is probably one of the commonest of all problems. While one or two stops may be understandable and even acceptable – for example if the horse has been asked to jump a fence from an impossible stride – refusing on a regular basis must be questioned. Discomfort or pain caused by saddlery or physical problems need to be checked out and remedied where applicable. Do not forget, either, that slippery ground, a rider with rough hands, or one who continually gets left behind and/or restricts the horse in the air, can quickly cause a crisis in confidence; no horse will keep jumping in such circumstances, or at least, only for a limited period of time. Sourness can also be a factor if the horse has done an excessive amount of jumping, as can the horse being over-faced. It is up to you, as the rider, to know how much it is fair to ask of your horse, and how often.

If you can eliminate these possibilities, you then need to ask the question: is it really the horse stopping at the fence, or is it the rider? If both horse and rider are confident you should not have a refusal, but if the rider is a little worried and subconsciously does not really want to jump a particular fence, he may well be rather half-hearted and the attitude will quickly communicate itself to the horse

If you have a refusal, try to analyse the reason why it happened so you can best decide how to deal with it. On this occasion, it was the first time this mare had been asked to jump a fence at this height and she wasn't on an ideal stride for it. However, her rider has tried hard to keep her moving forward from the leg up into the bridle while maintaining a very secure position. The numnah, commented on on page 63, has slipped back even further in this picture; sometimes, something like this can be responsible for causing a problem such as refusal to happen.

On the second attempt, the mare tackles the fence with confidence, if not the best style (she is standing off a little and could have brought her knees up higher).

through his actions. You must really want to jump that fence, and not just ride to it but be thinking in terms of riding over and to the far side of it too. When it comes to tackling bigger fences, some amateur riders are not perhaps so bold and confident as they imagine, even if the jumps are well within the horse's scope; if this is the case, the rider must be aware of his own limitations before it destroys the horse's confidence. Quite often, improving position and an eye for a stride will do a lot to help such problems, which inevitably arise through weakness in this area.

If a horse does stop, for whatever reason, it is not uncommon to see the rider re-approaching the fence at tremendous speed, and not always with a great deal of co-ordination; and if the horse

was not unduly worried about jumping before, he soon will be if ridden like this. It is far better to get the horse going forward again between hand and leg, and to re-approach with impulsion at a controlled pace, not at speed. All that happens by going faster is that the horse has less time to organize itself and adjust its stride and balance for a correct take-off; the rider is not really in control of the situation, even though he may think he is, and if the horse does stop again it will be far more unseating. By approaching steadily with the horse between hand and leg, it will be far easier for the rider to feel if the horse begins to prop, and he will have time and sufficient control to push the horse forward again into the rein contact with his legs. Do be prepared to lower the fence if necessary to get the horse going forward again, so that both it and the rider can regain confidence; it is as important for the latter as it is for the former, since a stop can shake a rider's nerve and weaken his resolve. Once both are going happily over the fence again, it can gradually be rebuilt.

It is true that some horses can be mickey-takers, so you do have to know your horse well and whether it is just trying it on or genuinely worried before you admonish it for refusing. If the horse refuses a fence of a type that it has not seen before, it is best to give it the benefit of the doubt the first time, and to introduce it quietly to a smaller version of the same obstacle. If you do feel a smack is justified, however, do not tickle the horse – which irritates it more – but give it a fairly sharp smack just behind your leg, taking your whip hand off the reins as you do so. When doing this, do not commit the common fault of restricting the horse with your hands, preventing it from going forward; even though it may shoot forward fairly rapidly, allow it to go forward at whatever speed it wants (within reason) and then gently steady it ten or eleven strides later. You have, after all, used your stick sharply to tell the horse to go forward, and that is what you must allow it to do, otherwise you risk confusing it. Do not hold the horse in front of the fence and hit it, either, as this can easily lead to the horse learning to rear. Turn the horse away, smack it, let it run on, then gently rebalance and steady it and approach your fence again.

RUNNING OUT

The reasons for running out can be the same as those for refusing: pain, the rider

being half-hearted, meeting the fence on a bad stride, asking the horse to jump a fence beyond its ability, or poor presentation. You may also find that the rider has dropped his hands on the approach and/or anticipated the fence and tipped forwards so that the horse has been given the opportunity to run out. With horses that run out, as with those that refuse, it can very often be the case that the rider does not subconsciously want to jump the fence anyway; the horse realizes this, the rider panics a little bit and lets the horse off the hook, and it then stops or runs out and consequently learns that it can get away with it.

If the horse does run out, always turn him in the direction it did not want to go; if it runs out to the left, for example, insist it turns to the right (even if it takes half an hour to achieve it) and then re-present the horse as soon as possible. It is

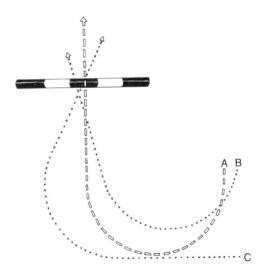

Riding a correct approach (a) and at an angle (b and c), which gives the horse the option of ducking out at a fence.

This is a fairly typical reaction from the rider when feeling the horse trying to run out: by using more left rein the rider has in fact made it even easier for the horse to duck out on its right shoulder. By keeping a firmer contact on the right rein and using more right leg she might have stood a better chance of getting over the fence.

A V of poles leaned against the front of a fence can be used to form a channel and prevent a horse from running out. When using this sort of arrangement, do not close up the angle of the V too much as it can be frightening for an inexperienced horse.

important to ride a correct approach: with impulsion, a correct contact, and straight, rather than at an angle; and check that you are sitting up, or even with your upper body very slightly behind the vertical so that you are able to keep the horse between hand and leg – although this should not mean that you get left behind in the air.

While it is possible to lean poles against the front of a fence to form a channel to prevent the horse from being able to run out, you are not going to have this sort of assistance when competing at shows, so why learn to rely on them at home? Far better instead to go back a few steps instead and jump a few smaller fences so that both horse and rider can regain any lost confidence and more control can be established.

DRIFTING IN THE AIR

This can be a difficult problem to solve as it is often caused by a physical problem in the horse, which could be anywhere between the head and the tail, and difficult to pinpoint without expert help. Investigate all the possibilities, teeth, back, and so on, but do get a specialist in the field to do this for you; while a vet in general practice may be very good at his job, he cannot be expected to be an expert on everything! One thing that many people often do not consider when thinking of physical problems is eyesight; like humans, horses can be long- or short-sighted, can have tunnel vision, impaired vision or be longer-sighted in one eye than in the other. Any of these defects could cause a horse to misjudge a fence or jump across it to one side, or indeed to start refusing.

However, if you can eliminate physical problems as a cause, there are several things you can do to try to correct it. Provided it is safe, you can use poles to encourage the horse to jump straighter across the fence. Straightness is a habit you want to encourage as much as possible, since drifting to one side will effectively make a spread wider, distances between fences awkward when jumping combinations and, depending on the amount of drift, may even tempt the horse to run out at successive obstacles. There is also a danger of the rider becoming injured by catching a leg or foot against a wing, or even pulling the fence over on top of the horse. In addition to using sloping poles across the front face of the fence or fences, you can also build verticals or spreads of cross-poles, even building up one side of it if necessary (the side towards which the horse tends to drift). Once the horse has hit it once or twice, it should have learnt its lesson and will begin to correct itself. Go back to your flatwork, too, as you can help to correct the horse by applying a little more leg on the side it drifts towards, and obviously this lesson of moving away from the leg as well as forwards from it needs to be well established on the flat before you can really use it to advantage over fences. Do try to avoid using your hands to correct the horse, though, as it can make the horse become very hollow, or even encourage it to stop eventually. Although in extreme cases you can give the horse a slap on the shoulder with your stick (on the side it drifts towards), it is not always the best policy as it is difficult to do this without interfering with the rein contact, and it can often make the horse worried and encourage it to speed up.

A sloping pole across the front of a fence to help keep a horse straight. Friday has got a little too close to the fence and has had to make a tremendous effort to clear it, tucking her legs back tightly beneath her, although she has dropped instead of raised her shoulder.

The rider also needs to be considered. If the horse has been consistently ridden by someone who leans to one side in the air, it will throw the horse off balance and make it drift. If the rider is crooked while jumping, it is quite likely that he will be when working on the flat or when out hacking, and this will lead to an uneven muscular development and one-sidedness. This problem may need some help from a person on the ground as it is not always easy to tell when you are sitting straight, even though you may be trying very hard to do so! With a horse that has become one-sided, it is important that small details, such as changing trotting diagonals, are not neglected, as this can otherwise contribute to the problem; although it may be harder work for both horse and rider, sufficient time must be spent on the more difficult rein.

LOSS OF IMPULSION BEFORE FENCES

Horses that are inclined to jump in this way – dropping behind the leg at the last minute, putting in an extra little stride and climbing over fences – are uncomfortable and lack fluency. They are usually the slightly stuffier ones who need more encouragement to go forwards; and they do not usually make the best showjumpers. This habit is often exacerbated if the rider is too passive, or tends to drop his hands, or tips forward on the approach; the rider needs to be positive and confident, sitting up and riding forward into a contact. The horse also needs to respond properly to the leg, so that if the rider feels the horse beginning to fade on the approach, he is able to close his legs and gain a correct and obedient response – and that involves work on the flat.

The fault can also stem from a lack of confidence, so you do need to know your horse. If it has a little, short stride and is lacking in scope, and you come into a fence and ask it to stand off, the horse will most likely attempt to fit in an awkward extra little stride, losing forward momentum and propping on to its forehand as it does so. This will be followed by an awkward jump, since the horse is lacking the power and engagement of its hocks to propel itself into the air. This does not necessarily constitute an evasion or naughty habit; the horse will do this because it is more comfortable (and probably safer) for it to tackle fences this way when confronted with such a problem. If this is the case, you must learn to judge your stride more accurately and be prepared to get that little bit closer to the base of each fence, rather than asking the horse to extricate itself by standing off, and losing all your fluency and impetus when it cannot manage it.

However, if your horse does not have an excessively short stride and yet begins to jump in this manner, it is quite likely that you have lost its confidence,

probably by misjudging the stride and take-off point. You must take steps to remedy this as quickly as possible, since the longer you allow it to continue the harder it will be to correct, and in the meantime the horse will be losing even more confidence and may begin to refuse.

Placing-poles in front of fences are excellent for sorting out this problem, provided, of course, that they are placed at a correct distance for the individual so that it is being asked to jump within its capabilities. Bringing the horse to a correct take-off point each time will increase the horse's confidence tremendously, as well as helping the rider to begin to see the correct take-off point more accurately. Do not forget, either, that hard ground can sometimes cause this problem, if the front legs become a little jarred up, so be sensible in your workload and prepared to ease up a little if necessary.

STANDING OFF

The problem of standing off fences is often related to stiffness, when the horse is not sufficiently athletic and supple to be able to get close to its fences and 'round' over them. Standing off is also related to rushing and lack of confidence. Sometimes it is not the horse's confidence in question, but the rider's. If the rider becomes too anxious and over-rides the horse the last few strides of an approach, it can encourage the horse to take off early; the rider must be confident enough to sit quietly, maintaining balance, rhythm and impulsion, and allow the horse to get closer. The problem can soon become a habit, and the more the rider anticipates the horse standing off and tries to ensure he is forward with it, the worse it gets. In such cases, it often helps to try to sit more passively and to visualize the fence moving towards you, rather than the other way round, so that the temptation to chase the horse towards it is lessened.

Where the habit is not caused by the rider, it is again a matter of knowing the horse before deciding how far to go in rectifying the problem. If the horse has been jumping like this for some years, and is successful, and provided he is not standing off a suicidal distance away from the fences, it may be best to leave well alone, especially if the horse is older and perhaps a little set in its ways.

However, it is worth bearing in mind that a horse that constantly stands off its fences has to put in a greater effort in order to make height and spread than one that can get closer and use itself more correctly in the air; also, as spreads become wider, it is more prone to catching a back rail with its hind legs, which is far more likely to frighten it (and lead to strain injuries) than catching a pole with the front legs on the way up. So with a younger horse, it is worth going back to basics and attempting to remedy matters. This will involve working on the flat to achieve an increased degree of suppleness and improved outline, and using placing poles in front of fences to produce a more athletic jump from a closer take-off point (*see* chapters on Flatwork and Gridwork).

It is also wise to have a vet examine the horse's back and hind legs, as a physical problem in these areas may mean that it is impossible for the horse to jump in an athletic style, and the veterinary report will help influence the course of action you take.

DANGLING FRONT LEGS

Young horses may often jump with loose, dangling front legs initially. As a result, they will jump higher than necessary to clear the obstacle. As a youngster becomes more experienced, and the fences gradually become bigger, it will learn to use its shoulders more and to lift its forearms and bend its knees, so that it does not need to overjump and can therefore be more economical with its energy. Work on the flat also helps to encourage the horse to engage its hocks beneath it more correctly, which enables it to lighten its forehand and use its shoulders more freely. To a certain extent, this will also help to improve the technique in front. Some horses, though, never learn to snap up their front legs correctly and continue to have to jump higher in order to compensate, which is fine provided they do not lose their confidence in doing so.

Trying to improve the situation then, involves flatwork primarily to encourage the shoulder to work more correctly, followed by concentrating on the lower leg (the cannons) by using a trot pole into fences and grids, in which the distances are gradually reduced. Use the open-fronted type of protective boots, so that when the horse does touch a pole it feels it and is more inclined to try to draw its knees up and fold its cannons back tightly out of the way the next time.

If the horse tends to dangle just a single leg, it is almost always the same one. This is a dangerous trait as it can so easily lead to a pole being caught between the front legs and tipping you both over. Check the offending leg very

A horse that does not tuck its legs up properly will have to jump higher in order to compensate. This mare is having to achieve considerably more height than should be necessary in order to clear the fence.

carefully as there may well be a physical problem – not necessarily high up, but even in the foot – which is responsible for this. If a physical cause cannot be found, use a pole set diagonally across the front face of a vertical (*see* drifting in the air, page 143) to try to encourage a better technique in that leg.

CATCHING POLES WITH THE HIND LEGS

This may well occur when the rider restricts the horse in the air with his hands. This prevents the horse from lowering its head and neck and thus from swinging the hind legs in an arc after the forehand over the fence. It can also happen if the rider gets left behind or sits up too early on landing (causing the horse to hollow and drop its quarters), or if the horse has stood too far off a spread and is unable to make the width.

It does sometimes happen because the horse is rather tight behind the saddle, but if the horse does begin to cramp up its back legs beneath itself, it is more usually a sign of lack of confidence or pain. It can be instructive to lunge the horse over some fences to see what it does when unhampered by the rider; if

Cramping: this was taken over the first part of a double and shows how positive you need to be. Quite often, the horse will be more concerned about the second part than the first, and is so busy looking at it that it can end up doing the most extraordinary things in the air. Ross's position is almost a recovery position as if he is uncertain that the horse is going to make it across the back pole – although in fact it did, and won the class.
(Photos courtesy of MVR Photographic.)

Trailing back legs. Some horses get very complacent if you keep fences too small for too long, as with this one here. She is making only as much effort as is needed, and is not really trying very hard – the front legs are very loose and the back ones trail badly.

By making the fence into a spread, the same mare is now having to make a better effort with her back end.

the style is better and the hind legs more correct, it is a fair assumption that the rider is the cause of the problem. If the hind legs are still awkward, do have them, and the quarters and back, examined by a chiropractor.

Catching poles with the hind legs is on the whole a rather more difficult problem to deal with than dangly front legs. It needs to be corrected by repetition and building up confidence, although never at the expense of making the horse bored and sickened. Build small but slightly wider spreads, encourage the horse to go forwards and allow complete freedom of the head and neck in the air; the back end should begin to follow through as the horse's confidence develops.

10 Summary

Using gridwork successfully lies ultimately in using your common sense, in knowing your horse – when to ask for more and when to call it a day, and in acknowledging its weaknesses as well as appreciating its strengths. 'Feel' plays an important role in judging your horse's progress and deciding upon what exercises to introduce and at what stage; you will always get feedback from your horse if you are prepared to be receptive to it. Do not just notice what the horse tells you, but be prepared to act upon it.

Obviously experience helps, but everyone has to start somewhere and it is hoped that the guidelines laid out in this book will provide that starting point. As you begin to develop an appreciation of how distances, and various types and combinations of fences all influence your horse differently, you will be able to expand and develop the exercises and ideas outlined here so that they are individually tailored to the needs and requirements of your horse.

It is, however, vital not to be too ambitious and attempt too much in each session, or even over a period of time. While some horses are very quick learners they do all have differing learning curves and some patience and restraint may need to be exercised – perhaps most of all with quick learners, when it can become tempting to hurry them. You must aim to maintain confidence at all times – a horse lacking in confidence will never be a good jumper – and when necessary be prepared to repeat earlier stages. Doing so is not an admission of failure, nor a poor reflection on your training, but rather a measure of your self-discipline and ability as a horseman to recognize when things are not going quite as they should, and to take immediate remedial steps before the situation escalates from a minor hiccup into a major problem. Taking a step or two backwards will more often than not save you more time in the long run and be more successful than persevering with your problems head on; and you will probably finish up with a better horse for having spent the extra time on it. While ambition can be a positive force, correctly utilized, it can prove to be disastrous if it leads to hasty, undisciplined, unstructured work and can ruin a potentially good animal.

Know not just when you yourself have achieved as much as possible in each session, but also when your horse has reached its limits. This can sometimes be difficult to assess, and this is when an experienced and impartial opinion is of benefit. Many top riders do give tuition (and at lower levels there are also many good instructors around), so do not hesitate to seek guidance if you feel you are getting stuck in a rut or experiencing difficulties.

We shall end on a note of warning: using gridwork does give the rider, as much as the horse, the confidence that he will always meet his fences correctly, but if used to excess it can create a certain amount of psychological dependence. A

151

little variety is no bad thing, anyway, so do jump courses and individual fences, too, so that you do not become too anxious when competing (when you will not have placing poles and so forth to assist you). Finally, remember that grid-work is a means to an end, not an end in itself.

Happy – and successful – jumping!

Appendix I

LOOKING TO THE FUTURE – AFFILIATION

As your horse's jumping training progresses, and you start to gain a few successes at shows, you might begin to think about competing in affiliated classes. One of the great advantages of this is that the courses are usually far better built and designed than those you will meet at unaffiliated shows. The courses are well organized, correct timing equipment is used, and the judges are experienced and approved.

Yet many riders seem to be unnecessarily daunted by the prospect. The strange thing is that these same riders will quite happily go and jump a less than inviting 1.1m (3ft 6in) track at unaffiliated shows, and even be very successful. Perhaps they are put off by the term 'affiliation', or simply do not realize that at the lower levels of affiliated competition, at any rate, the fences are frequently fairly low and the courses built to encourage fluency and confidence in both horse and rider.

In Britain, for example, at the bottom of the ladder are the British Novice Championship classes, where the fences are between 0.85m and 1m (2ft 9in and 3ft 3in) in height in the preliminary rounds. The fences are raised only very slightly in the jump-off so that inexperienced horses and riders are not overfaced. There are also various 'beginner' classes, produced by individual show centres, from which you can progress to Discovery, Newcomers and Foxhunter classes, all at sensible sizes and probably not beyond your scope if you compete successfully in unaffiliated Open classes.

In order to compete in affiliated classes in Britain, you must first become a member of the BSJA (British Show Jumping Association), which involves paying an annual subscription to the Association, plus an annual registration fee for each horse you wish to jump. The equivalent body of the BSJA in the USA is the American Horse Shows Association.

Apart from the subscription and registration fees, the costs of competing are pretty much the same as they are for unaffiliated shows: entry fees, travelling expenses, and so on. You do not need to be supremely gifted, or in possession of an exceptionally talented horse, in order to have a great deal of fun and a degree of success at the lower levels. A tremendous amount of satisfaction can also be derived from competing against well-known riders producing their up-and-coming youngsters through the same classes; and if you succeed in qualifying your horse, many of the finals are held at major international meetings, in Britain at the Royal International and Horse of the Year Show for example.

If you are still undecided about taking the plunge, go along to a local affiliated show as a spectator, and you may well be surprised to find the fences and courses at the lower end of the scale far less intimidating than you expected.

In Britain, further details and registration forms can be obtained from The British Show Jumping Association, British Equestrian Centre, Stoneleigh, Kenilworth, Warwickshire CV8 2LR. In the USA, contact American Horse Shows Association, 220 East 42nd Street, Suite 409, New York, NY10017.

Appendix II

BUYING JUMPS AND EQUIPMENT

Jumps and equipment can be found advertised for sale in local saddlers and in the classified pages of equestrian magazines. However, it is always advisable to go and look at them before ordering (and perhaps spending a lot of money) as quality can vary tremendously.

Some of the larger saddlery shops do stock Country Jumpkins and Bloks, as described in Chapter 6 (*see* page 83), but they can be ordered direct from the manufacturers:

Country Jumpkins
Baker-Mac
Denmill
Alford
Aberdeenshire
AB33 8EP
Tel and Fax:
  09755 62582

The Blok
Poly Prop
Siop Y Castell
Caerwedros
Llandysul
Dyfed
Wales SA44 6BW
Tel: 0545 560602

Index